FUSION: THE PSYCHOLOGY OF TEAMS

FUSION

THE
PSYCHOLOGY
OF TEAMS

DAVE WINSBOROUGH

For information, contact Hogan Press
11 S. Greenwood, Tulsa OK 74120
hoganassessments.com

ISBN: 978-0-692-98204-4

Interior Book Design by
MIchelle M. White Graphic Design

HOGANPRESS

*To Amanda and Finn with my
eternal thanks and love.*

Brooklyn, New York, June 2017

CONTENTS

PREFACE

More than 20 years ago, I transitioned from clinical psychology to organizational psychology. In part, the reason for this transition was that my clinical week required hours of listening to unhappy people share sad stories and struggle to make sense of their lives. I should be quick to point out that the work was noble, and, for the most part, that my patients worked hard to create a better existence. I particularly enjoyed the feeling that came from a therapeutic breakthrough, such as when someone began to feel happy after a long period of depression. In truth though, after nearly a decade of being professionally caring, I found it a dismal way to spend my days.

Around the time I was wondering about Plan B, two things happened. The first was an overseas conference, where I was introduced to the thinking of Robert Hogan, a bloke I'd never heard of, who was a big deal in the personality world. I found a book he had coauthored, called *Personality: Theories and Applications*, and, in the nicest possible way, became transfixed. The book was literate, scholarly, trenchant, and entertaining, and it led me through an adventure of ideas. It described the history of my field in ways that made sense of the welter of theories and studies that constitutes much of the muddy thought that flows from the towers of academic psychology. Hogan's thinking located individual human behavior in the context of groups and evolution and explained why we do the things we do. Looking back, I recollect the intense "Aha!" as my thinking fell into place, and the experience was transformative.

Second, I was presented with the opportunity to work with the survivors of an enormous corporate downsizing in the 1990s. These people were required to operate together under a new structure, but because they were having difficulty forming a cohesive whole, they requested some assistance with team building.

Team building was a trendy topic at the time, but I knew little about it, so I contacted both a high school gym teacher and a colleague of mine for advice. Working together, we designed a program for the new team. The program comprised completing a series of random field exercises while blindfolded, then retiring to a decrepit room attached to a motel to spend the next five or six hours disclosing information with one another, to build group cohesion and trust. It was surprisingly good fun, and I learned that I preferred working with happy people.

The team also enjoyed the activities, and declared themselves significantly improved. Sadly, their overlords disagreed, and about six months later, they were restructured out of existence. I, on the other hand, was launched on my new career.

Since then, I learned that any impact on that team was probably illusory: one-off team-building events rarely produce lasting improvement. But I followed my interest and became a diligent student of human evolution and group behavior. I have come to believe that human behavior derives its meaning solely from interaction with other humans.

> Working together to win—at war or work or mending a roof—is the simplest way to think about teams.

What you do while completely alone in the forest is more or less irrelevant, no matter how enjoyable or important it is to you. In contrast, how you behave with other people will influence your ability to build a career, form relationships, earn respect, and find meaning. Groups are the milieu in which humans act, and as Hogan points out, every interaction has an agenda, whether you acknowledge that fact or not.

Working together to win—at war or work or mending the roof—is the simplest way to think about teams. Humans evolved to work together because that strategy succeeds better than trying to do things alone. Without teamwork and an evolved sense of group identity, our ancient ancestors couldn't have built shelters, hunted big game, cultivated land, or defended against attacks and invasions from the tribe in the next valley.

Although we wear nicer clothes, drink better coffee, and use more machines than we did millennia ago, nothing has really changed regarding our reliance on others. Whether cleaning up after a devastating earthquake, building new software, running a big hedge fund, or managing the impacts of global warming, I assure you that working cooperatively is the only way to accomplish the task. The awe with which we attend to business winners like Elon Musk or Rajan Tata is alluring, but misplaced. All high achievers, from Genghis Khan to Queen Elizabeth I to Steve Jobs, relied on groups and teams to deliver on their behalf.

We laud solo achievement and mythologize heroic individual acts precisely because we perceive such acts as outliers, but the reality is that almost everything we do as a species is achieved through cooperation. In the same way a fish isn't aware of the water in which it swims, humans seem peculiarly blind to the wonder, power, and beauty of our *groupness*. This point explains why the typical organization handles teams so poorly. However, organizations' mishandling of teams has created opportunities for applied science to help people enjoy and perform more effectively in teamwork—in jobs, in sports, in community groups, and even in knitting circles.

This book explores the why, what, and how of better performing teams. Chapters 1 and 2 trace our human-family tree to understand the origin of our groupness, why it evolved, and how profoundly it is wired into our humanity. These first chapters also look at how and why the groupness of Homo sapiens differs from that of mole rats and wasps—very interesting, I promise you— and how warfare among groups drove a virtual arms race in team technologies, a race that is still going strong today. Knowing something about both the instinctive and the learned preference for working in groups will help readers become better at working with, and even leading, others, a topic that Chapter 3 addresses.

Extending this historical perspective, Chapter 4 reviews the impact of Western industrialization, which reified the role of the individual, and led Western corporations to forget how to work with teams and why teams are, more often than not, a natural work unit. Although almost 80% of organizations now employ teams, a machine-like view of human resources prevailed until recently, epitomized in Henry Ford's lament that when all he wanted was a pair of hands, the hands always came with a mind attached. The push for cost reductions, the need for role flexibility, the rise of knowledge work, the geographical distribution of company offices, and workers' preference for collaboration have driven a resurgence of interest in teams. Teams became officially fashionable again when Google announced the results of a multi-year investigation into high-performance teamwork, even though, as discussed later, the results were predictable and not innovative.

In Chapter 5 I outline my tripartite model of teamwork, the hard, the soft, and the deep factors that my consulting practice uses in thinking about and coaching working teams.

Chapter 5 also explores the hard design rules that underpin effective teamwork, which start with being clear about the outcome the team needs to deliver. Does that sound basic? It's not! Too frequently teams are presented as the solution when the problem hasn't been clarified. For example, teams are not always the most efficient way of accomplishing a particular task. Boiling an egg doesn't need teamwork. Idea generation may be either inhibited or enhanced when performed by a team. In short, because forcing people into meaningless teams leads to de-motivation and frustration, determining whether or not a given task will benefit from teamwork is the first step in applying the model. This chapter provides a simple tool to help users design a team that fits the task.

Chapter 6 introduces the more psychological, or soft, features of teamwork, which become more important after the hard factors are in place. Although group cohesion, trust, and psychological safety all boost teamwork, they don't, by themselves, lead to high performance. This point, though subtle, is nonetheless critical: cohesion, trust, and safety do not automatically lead to high performance, but they are required to achieve high performance.

Chapter 7 introduces a simple framework, called the Rocket Model, that joins the hard and the soft factors of teamwork. Not only does this model describe the requirements for building a high-functioning team, but it has the added benefit of being easy to remember.

Chapters 8, 9, and 10 dive into the deep water of the psychodynamics of teams. These chapters explain how to resolve issues among team members or why a group of skilled and competent players can fail to become a functioning team. The discussion uses the world of sports to explore the impact of personality on morale, relationships, and performance. For example, the collective meltdown of the French football World Cup team a few years ago demonstrates that personality affects team performance at least as much as ability does, if not more.

Research on personality and teams shows that the mix of personalities on a team can exert a profound influence on team performance. Bad apples—people who are moody, impulsive, poorly organized, and selfish—can produce catastrophic results.

To help structure thinking about the role of personality in teamwork, I explore personality in general and how personality affects the psychological roles people on teams play. For example, an accountant may play a specific role with the people around him or her—a driver for results, a social connector, or a hard-headed pragmatist—to name a few.

These chapters introduce the concept that values form the foundational glue for good teamwork. Shared values help teams bond. But at the same time, they may produce a homogeneity that leads to blind spots, like the one that occurred with John F. Kennedy's cabinet during the Bay of Pigs.

Equally, a team's dark side can produce cracks, or fault lines, in the structure and cohesion of the group. By "dark side," I mean the collective negative personality characteristics team members share; characteristics that lead to discord, distrust, and despair.

The three elements of roles, values, and fault lines comprise the Hogan Team Report (HTR), introduced in Chapter 11. Hundreds of teams have used this tool, which I developed with my colleague Gus McIntosh at Winsborough Limited in New Zealand, to explore the deep aspects of team functioning. The HTR holds up a psychological mirror to teams to help them understand their dynamics and plan strategies for improvement. It is designed specifically to reveal the psychology of the group and highlight areas for coaching. In Chapter 12 I describe the approach I have developed for using the HTR in team coaching, working through a number of case studies to show how to apply findings in the real world. Although the cases are real, the names of the companies are, of course, fictional.

I touch briefly on the difference between team building and team development. To be blunt, I advocate for the latter and disapprove of one-day team-building events. Nevertheless, because a certain body of evidence supports the value of team building, the chapter provides tools and interventions that might guide such a day.

On the other hand, as an unabashed fan of team coaching, I describe the process my company employs on our six- or 12-month engagements. The evidence for team development and team training in these engagements offers a compelling business case.

I should touch on a convention I adopt throughout the book. Simply, a group is a collection of people; they become a team when they have a shared task to achieve and clear boundaries about who is on or off the team. I tend to use both almost interchangeably, though I will lean towards teams.

In summary, the goal of this book is to share what I have learned about and from the many teams I have worked with in the last 20 years. I cannot help but compare it to clinical work. I reflect on the joy I get when working with people at their best and wanting to be better, and less frequently, at their collective worst, but still wanting to be better. I began my career by helping individuals overcome unhappiness, and I have progressed towards a more fundamental human endeavor—helping groups and teams and tribes do what comes naturally: work together.

1

IT'S JUST THE WAY WE ARE

*Society is something in nature that precedes the individual. Anyone who
either cannot lead the common life or is so self-sufficient as not to need
to, and therefore does not partake of society, is either a beast or a god.*

— Aristotle

The islands of New Zealand (NZ) are positioned astride the Pacific and Indo-Aus-
tralian tectonic plates, towards the very bottom of the Pacific Ocean. NZ anchors
the southernmost end of the Pacific Ring of Fire, and is so remote that it was the
last place on Earth to be colonized by human beings. One of the prizes for settling
last is that New Zealanders enjoy a beautiful, primal land—rugged mountains and
pristine lakes, miles of ocean-tumbled coastline, and green, rolling countryside.
On the other hand, the land itself is still forming. NZ contains a dozen live volcanoes
and experiences upwards of 12,000 earthquakes every year. In September 2010,
a monstrous 7.1-magnitude quake hit Christchurch, NZ's third-largest city, causing nearly $2.5 billion in damage, but, remarkably, no deaths. Five months later,
in February 2011, the city was again shaken in the middle of the working day by a
smaller 6.3-magnitude quake, a prolonged, shallow shaking that was technically
classified as an aftershock but caused greater devastation than the original quake.

New Zealanders gained an understanding of the word *liquefaction* as the ground
turned into a muddy jelly from the aftershock. Buildings and infrastructure damaged in the first earthquake slumped and tumbled into jumbled rubble during the
new quake. Water mains, sewer lines, and telephone and electricity lines were terribly damaged. Roads failed entirely, and schools and municipal services couldn't
operate. Many suburbs were cut off from utilities for months.

Already-weakened buildings in the central city folded like a house of cards. Christchurch, a beautiful city, was shattered and broken; it simply disintegrated. The cost of the devastation rose to a shocking $35 billion. One hundred eighty-five people lost their lives in the wreckage of toppled office blocks. Tens of thousands of homes were damaged beyond repair. Life in the city stopped and then returned to a primitive state, as people collected water from wells and taps in the street, cooked on grills, relied on outside sanitation, and called on friends and relatives for a place to shower. Authorities were unprepared for the scale of the calamity and for the magnitude of help that was needed.

During the days and weeks following the quake, armies of volunteers spontaneously emerged. Two armies formed: one, known as the Student Army, was made up of local university students; the other, dubbed the Farmy Army, comprised rural folks from the surrounding cropping, wool, and dairy farms. By the hundreds, these people brought shovels, trucks, wheelbarrows, food, clothing, and bedding, and gave their time and labor to help clean up the debris and assist those whose homes were destroyed.

Week after week, for months on end, these groups turned out, shoveling 200,000 tons of silt from roads, making and delivering hot meals, and providing camaraderie and support to earthquake survivors who were living in grief, squalor, and despair. These volunteers organized their efforts around the demands of their own lives and livelihoods for strangers they had never met and communities they had never visited.

An earthquake is an extraordinary event. Mission and urgent need will get a team started, but coordination at the scale of the Farmy Army and the Student Army cannot be sustained indefinitely. As with all human groups, hierarchy and specialized functions emerged to make the two groups effective and to channel their drive and effort. Both the armies developed relatively formal communication systems, financial and logistical operations to house and distribute supplies, and schedules and rosters to match skilled individuals and small teams with specific tasks. In other words, they developed a hierarchy, a division of labor, and organization. A few people led, most followed, and each individual found a particular way to contribute according to ability. Both groups invented a name and a brand identity for members to distinguish themselves and developed a powerful sense of camaraderie and connection.

This story is not unique in human history. Of course people band together to help each other in times of crisis; of course they personally make an effort to help strangers, even when they receive no tangible reward. Most helpers explain their actions by saying something to the effect of, "Well, we have to make the effort! We hope people would do the same for us if the tables were turned."

But this mutual, cooperative spirit turns out to be remarkably rare in the animal kingdom. Even though there are plenty of examples of group-dwelling animals, none behave anything like the way the New Zealanders exhibited cooperation and coordination. Lions and orcas will hunt together and remain in packs for their own protection and for the protection of their offspring. Elephants and dolphins care for others who are hurt. But in most animal groups, the intimacy of social life also involves competition for resources, whereby individuals vie with one another for food by scrambling to eat first or fighting to take the food away.[1] Dominance is a sound strategy, and individualism is ultimately what motivates animal behavior.

Compare the mammalian world with a form of life that thrives in more places and is numerically more abundant than anything living on Earth except bacteria: ants. Ants (and wasps and termites) are anti-individualists. Instead, they are super-cooperators whose entire social structure promotes the success of the group over that of the individual. Single ants owe their survival not to their own food-hunting prowess, but to the remarkable social structure of the colony. Individuals assume roles—soldiers, workers, nursery attendants, queens, farmers—roles that are more rigid than their counterparts in human society, but are in thrall to the needs of the collective. Their strategy is so effective that the famous biologist, E. O. Wilson, points out that ants are the dominant species of the microhabitats they occupy, pushing other insects and small animals to life at the margins.[2] Although it is a hard notion to grasp, Wilson considers the colony as the organism, rather than the myriad tiny beings which make it up. The ant approach to life is so unusual in nature that only 20 species of animals exhibit it. But eusocial (the scientific term for super-cooperators) animals are so wildly successful that while they comprise only a tiny fraction of the known species on Earth, they contribute about 50% of Earth's biomass.

Humans are the ants of the mammalian world. Whereas wolf packs consist of a dozen individuals at most, humans coexist in hundreds of millions, occupying complex nests (cities). Humans have specialized workers to take care of nurseries, building, and food supplies; moreover, as the plethora of wars has demonstrated, not only are humans prepared to defend their nests vigorously, they also sacrifice themselves altruistically for that cause. So fruitful has human beings' cooperative approach been that we now dominate the earth entirely, for better or worse. Scientists even invented the term *ultra-sociality* to differentiate animal eusociality from human super-cooperation.

Beyond that, we have developed distinctive tribal cultures that encode the lessons and knowledge that our ancestors accumulated. The anthropologist Joseph Henrich even describes culture as the collective brain of the tribe.[3] By that, he means that the ability of human groups to remember what others have learned through countless generations, and passed on, like fire, levers, the wheel, screws, cooking, writing, and, importantly, institutions (like armies, courts, or the press) is more powerful than innate intelligence. Henrich's view is that these cultural artifacts (the wheel lead to mass transportation, for example) actually alter us physically and psychologically, making us even more group-dependent.

If you like, you can perform a quick thought experiment to check Henrich's notion that we are now dependent on accumulated cultural knowledge to survive: imagine that a plane crash left you the sole survivor, washed up on a deserted island. You are now without the internet, power, toilets, or the knowledge to extract food, water, clothing, and shelter from the resources on the island. No matter how intelligent you are, without specialist cultural knowledge, how long will you live?

A grounding in human eusociality is fundamental to understanding human teamwork. Our banding into groups and teams and our penchant for coordinating individual efforts towards a common end didn't happen because such banding feels warm and sentimental (although we sometimes have those feelings when communing with our friends and relatives). Nature allows only the fittest animals to survive and thrive. In this light, teamwork developed as an evolutionary weapon that enabled people who banded together to survive. Successful collaboration allowed those early humans who mastered cooperation to survive against a tough African environment and to withstand attacks from other groups who wanted their resources.

We acquired our ultra-sociality via two major evolutionary steps. First was the "berry gathering" step. Individuals could forage larger amounts of food, like berries, if they worked together rather than alone. Because collaboration led to greater reward than individual competition did, those bands who practiced it grew fatter, richer, and raised more children.

This collaborative strategy even extended to helping someone at no gain to oneself. You can see it every day in tiny ways, such as giving directions to a lost and bewildered stranger on a city street. Such behavior does not really exist in the animal kingdom. For example, primatologist and psychologist Michael Tomasello points out that it is inconceivable to see two chimps carrying a log together to make a bridge to cross a stream. Furthermore, chimps have never been observed to teach each other anything at all. Thus, when people began to create and defend campsites, they extended the capacity for social coordination way beyond that of other primates.

During the slow millennia of human evolution, cooperative group living evolved as the most effective response to the challenging environments in which early humans lived. Human beings thrived precisely because they joined together to find food, bring down wild game, defend against attack from competing tribes, and share the burdens of child rearing. The personality psychologist Robert Hogan argues that the capacity for getting along with others became a hard-wired characteristic of human personality. Teams emerge from our very nature and are our most basic working structure.

The second evolutionary leap was the "branded knowledge" step, or the accretion of culture. It occurred when shared ways of doing things, deep knowledge of specific tools or techniques, religious beliefs, rules, and institutions differentiated one group from another. One's own group, with its familiar rituals, habits, and name, automatically became associated with everything right and good, whereas that other group, with its weird beliefs and barbaric traditions, was automatically bad. Such distinctions created deep shared identities among group mates and either created real advantages in the battle of life, or the group disappeared from the gene pool. Similarly, if your crew had access to better spear throwing technology than the opposition, the chances were good that you got the best hunting grounds. This identification with a culture is easily visible today, in the form of allegiances to sports teams, clothing, or technology brands, and, of course, religious and political groupings.

In addition to the berry gathering and branded knowledge steps, we evolved psychological concepts like fairness, justice, and reciprocity as ways of regulating individual behavior to promote the well-being of the group. These forms of social controls differ from those of other primates, and certainly distinguish humans from ants and other eusocial insects. Ants don't have courts of appeal. Fairness doesn't cut much ice in chimpanzee society. Wasps don't, by nature, reciprocate. People, by contrast, began to appreciate—to emotionally feel—that to be a good member of the group, one must not only be helpful and fair, but also conform and defend against whatever threatens the collective, including cheaters within the group. In this way, human morality became fundamentally wired into our groupness. A moral sense of the right way to behave—meaning to cooperate and help, as the Farmy Army did—became core to human psychology and individual identity.

So, from a behavioral adaption, teamwork evolved as a deeply rooted way of thinking and being for humans, and in ways that were different to the reflexive cooperation of ants. With that grounding in mind, the next topic examines how evolutionary roots still influence modern teamwork.

THE ANCIENT FOUNDATIONS OF ALL GREAT TEAMS

No man can outwit the ancestors

African proverb

It was by no means guaranteed that Homo sapiens would thrive. That they have is due to uncountable ancestors who evolved a social technology so powerful that it ultimately rendered humans all but invincible, enabling them to create vast and complex nests (cities) that operate on the shared notion of getting along with countless others, few of whom they actually know. Collaborating with each other, people created progressively more productive technologies. They copied, expanded, and refined the inventions and work of others to such a level that no other species, except viruses, can threaten them in any meaningful way.

The distinction between groups and teams is worth a quick mention at this point. Researchers get terribly hung up on this distinction, but in the real world, the difference is quite straightforward. Golfers play in groups, but football players play in teams. One hunter might track and bring down a squirrel, but a team is required to bring down a mastodon. Teams cannot achieve their tasks without coordinating and cooperating with others. In contrast, groups complete their tasks as individuals.

Although it has taken millions of years of development to get here, in fact only three adaptations altered patterns of human thought, emotion, and behavior from the typical primate model and moved it towards today's ultra-social human model. These three are: shared intentions, in-group bonding, and leadership and followership. While these changes sound simple, don't underestimate them, as they liberated and supercharged our ability to team. We'll explore them one by one below.

1. SHARED INTENTIONS

The traditional Victorian English puppet show called *Punch and Judy* is a popular, and typically violent, British boardwalk offering. During a *Punch and Judy* performance, Judy looks innocently into the audience of children while Punch is malevolently sneaking up behind her with a stick. The young audience immediately understands what is about to happen and calls out (audiences have a key role in the fun) to warn Judy that Punch is behind her with evil intentions.

The kids quickly understand Punch's intent—his future actions. Grasping another person's thoughts and intentions before they do something may not sound terribly important, but that singular ability marks the dividing line between human and animal intuition. For example, two elephants standing together and looking longingly at an out-of-reach branch laden with fruit will do nothing spontaneously; conversely, two humans will work together to get the fruit—one will hold down the branch while the other strips off the fruit. Cooperation at the level that humans practice it requires a shared sense of what we are about.

The central element of people's unique ability to cooperate is a capacity and motivation for shared intentionality. Humans have evolved to share goals, information, and tasks; most other animals have not, or not to anywhere near the same degree. Humans are hardwired to understand what others intend, and we have mental equipment that allows us to read their needs and moods, and to cooperate with each other.

 Michael Tomasello has spent years comparing the behavior of human infants and chimpanzees to better understand cooperation. In a series of experiments, he showed that both chimps and young children understood that when a person pointed towards a key, it was to help them unlock a puzzle box and claim a reward.[4] But when that person needed help to find a key, it was only the human children who offered assistance by pointing. Chimps did not point to help the person in the lab, and they don't point for one another in the wild.

Humans, more than other primates, have developed sophisticated neural circuitry that allows them not only to mimic others' actions, but to mimic others' mental and emotional states.[5] That capability allows us to form a pretty clear idea of what others feel, what they want, and what they intend to do. For thousands of generations, the sharing of each other's thoughts and objectives has allowed humans to co-ordinate more effectively and on a much larger scale than other animals do, by facilitating better defense, attacks, food gathering, and group movement.

It has also made warfare and competition between tribes radically more lethal. Charles Darwin found this point appealing when he noted in *The Descent of Man* that the tribe with many members who are always ready to give aid to each other and who sacrifice themselves for the common good will be victorious over other tribes.

Without shared awareness, shared goals, or shared plans, coordinating is impossible. Shared intentionality is the sine qua non of teamwork—having a mental representation of what we need to do and how we need to do it is the essential building block of cooperative work.

THE POWER OF SHARED INTENTIONS AT IBM NEW ZEALAND

Sometimes it is easier to understand the impact of something when it's not present. For example, have you ever struggled in a team that had no shared sense of purpose, or where members were at cross-purposes? In 2000, Nick Lambert came from outside the traditional IBM hierarchy to take over as the general manager of IBM NZ. At that time, the company had just extricated itself from a botched project with the NZ government; its reputation was in tatters, staff engagement was miserably low, and red ink dripped steadily from the P & L.

Worse, IBM's management structure made untying the Gordian Knot look easy. Lambert took the helm of an organization in which his senior line managers reported to bosses in Asia, America, and Australia, while remaining on a dotted line relationship to him. This meant he rarely had formal authority over them. Meanwhile, they competed with their colleagues for customers, sabotaged each other's business plans, created their own marketing and sales activities, and avoided meetings with impunity. Lambert's first leadership team meeting took place around a long board table with 25 people who sat with laptops open, answering emails while studiously ignoring one another and their new boss.

Lambert knew that his first objective was to have this group put aside their selfish interests and coordinate their efforts for the common good—that is, to mold the group into a cohesive team. He also knew 25 people act more like a knitting circle than a management team. Nonetheless, he was surprised by the energy required to create that team; his employees simply saw no need to work together. The situation was more dire because Lambert had been told that if the NZ operation wasn't fixed within a 24-month period, it would be run as a side operation from Australia.

Rather than focus on the dysfunctional team, Lambert worked with my firm to instill a strong sense of mission in the next level of younger leaders. Using the movie, *The Matrix*, as a dystopian allegory for the daily reality of IBM corporate life, we invited them to a program of secret midnight retreats with Lambert, a large, charismatic figure; loose, relaxed planning sessions; and finally, a formal program of change, all with the aim of rescuing the company from inertia and factional infighting. This engendered a strong, shared revolutionary purpose which resulted in nothing less than rebuilding the business (escaping the matrix) and saving IBM's reputation in NZ. The group adopted a name and a revenue goal: The Billion Dollar Babies (BDBs). The BDBs set about evangelizing a new way of operating inside the company via raucous events, spreading formerly seditious ideas ("a single voice to the customer"), and having a good time.

Over the next 12 months, three things occurred. First, the BDBs seized on the matrix theme and deeply bonded over their mission. The group was incredibly energized by the trust shown in them and became good friends and strong supporters of each other, even when competing for the same promotion. Second, the existing tier of leaders was initially bemused by the rumors about the BDBs (which was our intent), then gradually miffed at being excluded; they clamored to be involved and not left behind. Third, when Lambert felt he had momentum on his side, he cut the top team from 25 to 10 and promoted some of the BDBs to senior roles, creating a super-tight team committed to a strong purpose and to supporting each other. Two years later, staff morale soared and the NZ firm had begun to win back customers and contracts. By the time Lambert left, three and half years later, IBM NZ had moved from losing nearly $100 million a year to posting fat profits.

The IBM story shows not just that shared intentions are vital for teamwork, but that they cannot simply be imposed from above. It is better to present groups with a problem to puzzle over and solve than drop a target on their heads. Revenue goals were already mandated for Lambert's existing team, but without a felt individual

commitment, a shared identity, and shared intentionality, goals in and of themselves lack passion. Humans will revert to pursuing their own selfish interests
in the absence of an emotional connection powered by purpose. Similarly, they
tend not to volunteer their energy without a reciprocal autonomy and trust, a lesson ignored by autocratic micromanagers but one that every aspiring team leader
should grasp. We'll look at the power of bonds next, and some examples of har-
nessing them to produce powerful team outcomes.

2. IN-GROUP BONDING

If shared intentionality is essential, then it is underpinned by an even more primal emotion: the intense, clannish desire to be part of a group. This desire to mark
oneself as belonging was why we made sure Lambert's group of young managers
adopted a name for themselves (the Billion Dollar Babies) and defined for themselves a mission, which was revolution, á la *The Matrix*.

People frequently suggest that modern-day sport is only a slightly more civilized
substitute for tribal warfare, and that watching sports satisfies a need to connect
and bond. People want to watch their team, who are the good guys, trounce the
other team, who are the bad guys. The tens of thousands who turn up at stadia
across the globe go there because it is an intense group experience. They go to
lose themselves in the crowd and to generate and share intense emotions—to
chant, cheer, sing, experience ecstatic communion, generate commitment (to a
political cause, for example) together. The same motive drives rock concerts, religious services, or even riots. Some years ago, I vividly recall protesting against a
rugby tour of New Zealand by the national team of South Africa, who had banned
black players from eligibility. The police and tour supporters fought battles with
the marchers in the streets outside game venues over the whole five weeks of
the tour. For the most part, the protests were peaceful, but on occasion they devolved into tense standoffs or even pitched battle. I found a fierce joy running
with a crowd, chanting, and standing shoulder to shoulder with my (unknown)
protestor colleagues.

In fact, spectating has occurred during real battles; for example, during the
American Civil War, more than 500 people attended the First Battle of Bull Run
to watch the Union and Confederate armies fight. According to Hennessy, these

bystanders "were all excited, especially one woman with an opera glass. A hand-ful of soldiers made their way among the spectators, offering commentary and interpretation."[6]

These examples show that it is almost impossible to overstate how deeply wired our identification with groups is, although for the most part, we rarely see our parti-sanship and bias for what it is and we certainly ignore its negative consequences, such as racism or ethnic conflict. A philosopher once asked, "What is the differ-ence between society and the sun?" The answer is, "If you really want to, you can stare directly at the sun, but to see society, you must use special glasses."[7] It's very hard to observe the milieu in which one exists.

Running psychological experiments is one way to put on special glasses. A well-known psychological study, the summer camp experiment run by Muzafer Sherif in 1954, illustrated this point by testing between-group conflict.[8] Sherif brought two groups of preteen boys to an Oklahoma camp for a typical American summer experience. However, he kept the groups, yet unaware of each other's existence, apart for a few days to allow bonding. Even though they thought they were alone, each group created a distinct identity (the Eagles and the Rattlers) and started marking out its territory.

After six days, the Rattlers uncovered evidence that the Eagles had been play-ing baseball on their baseball ground. The Rattlers challenged the Eagles to a game, which was the start of a week of competitions, which Sherif had planned from the start.

Sherif and his researchers were amazed by what emerged. The competitions seemed to have triggered a circuit in each boy's brain, and Sherif saw that any activity with a chance to become competitive (pitching a tent, baseball, etc.) was entered into with more zest and speed. Tribal identity was also expressed when-ever and wherever possible: making flags to hang in the other's territory, wear-ing distinctive war paint, creating group chants. Finally, the two groups' activities escalated to hostilities, as they raided each other's bunkrooms, called each other names, and even made weapons from socks filled with rocks.

The connection between warfare and sport highlights just how primal the group mentality is. For example, a Pacific team will often perform an ancient war dance in front of the other team before a game starts. Originally designed to scare opponents and call down help from the god of war, the most famous of these is the *haka* of the New Zealand All Blacks, a rugby team. Sitting in the stands when a haka is performed is spine-chilling; facing a haka on the field can terrify the opposition. When a New Zealand team performs an awesome haka, the dance creates ecstasy in onlookers—every able-bodied individual present wants to leap onto the field and rend the enemy limb from limb. Social psychologist Jonathan Haidt suggests we enter a hive mind at these times, losing our individuality and experiencing mass connection and a dramatic lift in our spirits.[9] He thinks this phenomenon is especially strong in modern sports arenas, but that it also occurs during protests, marches, dances, concerts, and even in church. Wherever human groups gather and get excited, angry, or ecstatic, the resulting spirit is primitive, real, and as strong as it ever was.

In an ingenious series of experiments that sought to test the outer limits of our clannish nature, one of the most eloquent researchers in this area, Henri Tajfel,[10] demonstrated just how instinctive and emotional group identity is. Tajfel showed schoolboys pictures by the 20th century artists Paul Klee or Wassily Kandinsky and asked the boys which painter they preferred. The paintings themselves were irrelevant; Tajfel just wanted the boys to make a forced choice. They were then asked to distribute money to two unseen and unknown schoolboys, one of whom shared their painter preference and one who preferred the other painter. Even though the grouping was randomly assigned, the boys still favored their unseen, unknown in-group mate. The human preference for those who are like us, and the rejection of those who are not like us, is swift, instinctive, and unconscious. We are hardwired to identify with our group.

We have seen above that cooperation depends on shared intentions and that cooperative behavior allowed our ancestors to concentrate on hunting high-risk, high-reward game animals, like the mean-spirited, four-meter curved horned Pelorovis antiquus, the ancestor of modern cattle. The ability to hunt and bring home larger prey meant that hunter-gatherer bands were able to grow larger as well. The groups who were best able to coordinate big hunts and most effective in distributing food among the tribe outperformed those who were uncoordinated or who fought to keep what they killed (like chimpanzees still do).

3. MORALITY

Although cooperation might work well for the group, it can become a risky strategy for the individual: to the degree that an individual behaves selflessly, others may take advantage of that person's good nature by taking his or her share. In the fruit tree example I used earlier, in which two people instinctively worked together, the risk would be that the person who stripped off the fruit simply walked away and left the person who had held down the branch with nothing to eat.

Evolutionary psychologists call this cheating behavior freeriding. Hiding when your bandmates are attacked, claiming your share after a hunt, when in reality, you snoozed under a tree, and letting someone else do the cooking all the time are attractive individual strategies—they allow you to ride for free on someone else's labor. After all, why risk getting killed? Why work harder?

Because if you don't pull your weight, you can't stay in the group. While we band together to gain something like protection of food, we also stay to avoid ostracism or rejection. On the ancestral plains of Africa, being ejected from the group and left alone pretty much equaled a death sentence.

People are hardwired to feel afraid of rejection. For example, housemates object to one roommate not doing his or her share of the work. Typically, resentment builds a consensus against the shirker through gossiping behind his or her back. Soon, though, the housemates will gang up on the shirker and try appeals to fairness or to group rules. If that doesn't work, they will begin shaming. And if that doesn't work, they'll reject the lazy housemate or even kick the shirker out of the apartment. All group culture operates according to this dynamic: a system of rules and beliefs to balance the needs of individuals against the needs of the group. It might be thought of as a constitution for what it means to be human. You have the *right* to share in group success and the *obligation* to defend the group and treat others fairly.

To test how hardwired the unwritten rules that encourage conformity are, just try to break a taboo against, for example, food stealing. The next time you are eating at a restaurant, get up in the middle of your meal, walk over to someone else's table, grab a spoon, and take a hearty bite out of their mashed potatoes. Or test the taboo about ratting on your teammates: at a team project review, stand up in front of everyone and tell the boss that you delivered the project by yourself, that your teammates were completely useless, and that you alone deserve all of the bonus money.

We dislike cheats and resent those who don't pull their weight. We dislike those who dominate and gain unfair advantage. Our most basic psychology encompasses mental and emotional mechanisms that make us physically uncomfortable if we violate an unwritten rule. The same feelings alert us to transgressions by others, and even by ourselves, that harm the interests of the group.

Human beings have quite strong physical and emotional reactions when social norms are ignored or violated. Every day, we follow unwritten rules that make fitting in easier and smoother: standing in line, politely listening to someone's ideas in a meeting, returning a wallet found on the street. We don't *have* to do those things, but the act of breaking one of these rules leaves most of us feeling bad about ourselves: ashamed, which is the internal sense of transgression, or embarrassed, which is when others know what you did, because we care deeply about our reputations.

People are quick to punish deviation from the rules. In fact, economic studies have shown people will relinquish rewards and even pay for the chance to punish someone who cheated them.[11] This penchant is a clue to one of the strongest mechanisms humans use to promote conformity within the group: gossip. Gossip can be thought of as an ongoing evaluation of someone's status, trustworthiness, and competence. No matter what you think of magazines like *People, Us Weekly*, or *OK!*, they serve a purpose. Gossip fills a vital role in human group life and serves as an early warning system about the existence of a cheat, a bully, or someone who unscrupulously used others to meet their own needs. Gossip is also an important tool to bring someone down to size without physical force ("Have you heard what they are saying about you?"). If reputations didn't matter in human society, then EOnline, Twitter, and Facebook wouldn't wield the power they do.

Jonathan Haidt suggests that the strictures and taboos described above are engrained in five "moral flavors" that operate as an unconscious guide for how to act inside the group.[12] Evolution has co-opted humans' emotional circuits to nudge individuals into conformity, thereby helping the group to remain cohesive and generally cooperative.

TABLE 1. THE MORAL FLAVORS

	LOYALTY VS BETRAYAL	FAIRNESS VS CHEATING	AUTHORITY VS REBELLION	CARE VS HARM	SANCTITY VS DEGRADATION
Adaptive challenge	Staying together in the face of threats to the group.	Promoting in-group food sharing and cooperative effort.	Using leadership and followership as a group resource.	Protecting and caring for infants and young.	Avoiding impurities and disease.
What it delivers to the group	Commitment to the group effort. Promotion of group outcomes over individual desires.	Discourages cheating & deception; reduces freeriding. Emphasizes the benefits of being in the group.	Produces deference to wisdom and legitimate authority. Regulates dissent and enhances group effectiveness.	Keeps the group's future alive. Fosters preparedness to share the burden of long childhood and adolescence.	Accumulation of knowledge about pro-health practices.
Emotional response	Group pride, belonging, rejection.	Feeling obligated and wanting to reciprocate, or feeling anger, shame, embarrassment.	Respect or resentment.	Compassion.	Smugness, cynicism, disgust, revulsion.
Modern triggers	Sports, wars, work teams.	Strong individual moral code, bank fees, income tax reports, excessive compensation packages.	Respected leaders, political leaders, warlords.	Big-eyed cartoon characters, big-eyed infants like baby seals.	Prosocial movements or negative ideologies. Think gun control, racism.

Of course, people differ in the extent to which they respond to their moral taste buds. As an example of how to use them, consider the way the morality emerged in our work with IBM:

THE MORAL FLAVORS AT IBM NEW ZEALAND

Nick Lambert understood that demanding loyalty is a contradiction in terms. Expecting immediate loyalty and commitment from the existing leaders was pointless. He knew they had zero reason to feel committed to him, so his decision was to build a group of next-generation leaders who shared an understanding of both the imminent threat and their own future potential if successful. This group bonded tightly and shared their story about change and renewal across the company. Instead of the usual cynicism about IBM's arcane bureaucracy, they talked about their pride in the company and the need to do the right thing. Their commitment and personal example helped others pull together towards a common cause. The loyalty/betrayal theme meant that cooperation was suddenly hot and lone-wolf operators were not.

The authority/rebellion theme played a role in the change strategy as well. The movie *The Matrix* had recently been released, and its iconography provided a metaphor for the changes Lambert wanted to drive. At company events, Lambert adopted the persona of Morpheus and invited staff to choose between staying the same or waking up. The Billion Dollar Babies felt rebellious, yet were a positive force for renewal in a tightly run organization.

Finally, the fairness/cheating theme emerged in discussions among senior leaders. Customers carried a deep sense of distrust stemming from turf wars and sketchy deals in which IBM's current leaders had sold large projects by offering significant discounts on another leader's product. Lambert continuously strove to promote the law of abundance—if we work together to score huge customer wins, petty disputes about bonuses and discounts will become irrelevant. In other words, work together to be so successful that you won't care what the other guy makes.

These culturally acquired sentiments accelerated human development towards more teamwork. It is important to understand the word "sentiment" in this context; sentiment implies feeling committed to the group more than just thinking oneself committed. If life were a football tournament, it's the difference between turning out for your club week after week, dressed in club colors and singing your lungs out versus falling asleep in front of the TV while the game is on. In this way, the best teamwork is a profoundly emotional activity, and the ups and downs of team performance are experienced in a visceral way.

Cultures matter, of course, which is why Lambert sought to re-establish norms of cooperation at IBM. As individuals, we have all sorts of strengths and weaknesses, but collectively we are capable of arriving at solutions that would elude any single one of us. A controversial theory holds that cultures actually began to change the way we evolved. As Joseph Henrich posits, it is very likely that this ability to curate and pass on information began to change our brains physically by making them larger, and psychologically by making us super-cooperative. Henrich's idea is called The Cultural Brain Hypothesis:[13]

One generation adds a few things to it, the next generation adds a few more things, and the next generation, until it's so complex that no one in the first generation could have invented it. This was an important line in human evolution; . . . this is the idea that the real driver in the expansion of human brains was this growing cumulative body of cultural information, so that what our brains increasingly got good at was the ability to acquire information, store, process and retransmit this non-genetic body of information.

Groups that perfected methods and tools for living, and who sustained and enhanced those methods over generations, outperformed and outcompeted those who failed to work together in the moment and over time. The most basic fact of our collective psychology is that we are highly social; the second is that effective groups develop cultures that encode the wisdom of the ages.

As evolution locked down shared intentionality and group bonds as prerequisites for more effective teamwork, people began to employ their groupness as a tool across many different environments and tasks. The other adaptation that emerged turned out to hold the key that could unlock great team performance: leadership. We explore that adaptation next, in its own chapter.

LEADERSHIP AND FOLLOWERSHIP

Leadership is a potent combination of strategy and character.
But if you must be without one, be without the strategy.

— Norman Schwarzkopf

My son, Finn, worked part-time at a petrol station after school. Three or four people worked the shift, and the tasks were pretty mundane—greet customers, pump gas, take payment, sell coffee and snacks, stock shelves, clean the restrooms, and so on. In fact, the training manuals standardized the tasks involved in each service. After just a few weeks of working at the station, the shift crew had developed a predictable, straightforward routine.

This routine was interrupted when management trainees arrived for their front-line supervisor service experience. As Finn pointed out:

> These people arrive and suddenly start issuing orders, giving us pep talks, and trying to improve our routines. They don't even know the job. It's a two-week period of little Hitlers, and we have to keep the place running while they lead. Even regular customers roll their eyes at the behavior.

Leadership is the third great adaptation that promotes effective group behavior. Nevertheless, as the petrol story illustrates, leadership can be inept or bad, just as it can be good. Perhaps leadership is a little like salt for cooking: not enough, and the dish is bland and tasteless; too much, and it's inedible. Robert Kaiser, a well-known authority on leadership development, and Robert Hogan have written together extensively about the evolution of leadership. They suggest that a collaborative leadership style and an egalitarian group culture characterized human groups for roughly two million years before farming and cities developed.

Their point is well borne out by studies conducted with some of the last remaining hunter-gatherer societies on Earth. Christopher Boehm, an anthropologist who has lived with a number of these tribes, points out that not just the best hunters and toughest warriors get to be leaders. Tribal leaders need to be trusted, respected, and experienced in the relationships inside the group. Boehm notes that bullies can arrive at the top but are rarely successful leaders over the longer term, as the rest of the tribe typically conspires to undermine a domineering boss. Boehm describes a "reverse dominance hierarchy," in which power depends on the rank-and-file tribe members' deciding whether or not to follow a leader. Among the Yanomamo of Venezuela and Brazil, he observed villages breaking up when enough followers got sick of a domineering bully and decided to set up a new encampment on their own.

> Leadership evolved as a resource for group success.

So, as Finn wondered, if leadership isn't essential, what's it really for? Recall that effective group living requires that the members cooperate to hunt game or defend against an attack. Good leaders leverage shared intentions by generating goals, tasks, and direction, and by making sure hunters don't bicker over where to hunt. In modern teams, good leaders help everyone understand the path forward. If that path is clear, or the task simple and well understood, then leadership simply gets in the way. In Finn's case, the procedures were so well established and followed that close monitoring wasn't necessary.

Obviously, teaming is compromised when no one wants to follow; if the hunters scatter their separate ways because their leader is inept or difficult to get along with, they cannot track, kill, and bring back large game. Good leaders understand that followership is a *rational* strategy—that is, leaders must make sure that their approach benefits everyone.[14] Followers in well-led groups do better than those in poorly led groups or in groups that too frequently disagree. The trade-off is that followers have a legitimate expectation that leaders will act with their interests at heart and take the needs and feelings of team members into account.

Leadership exists to promote the success of the group. Leadership evolved as a resource for *group* success and survival. After all, it was not the fittest individuals, but rather the fittest bands, tribes, and clans that survived in our ancestral past.

The key task for a leader is getting individuals to put aside their selfish interests for the sake of the team goal.

In the 1960s, the leadership theorist John Adair used a similar insight in creating his elegant three-circle model describing what good teams need: tasks, members, and a shared identity and structure.[15] He developed the model for the British Army in the 1960s, but it holds up well even now. His basic point is that teams are functional. That is, they only exist in order to achieve something that an individual cannot do or would take too long to do. Adair felt strongly that individuals work best on tasks that are meaningful and challenging. The team needs motivated individuals who possess the right skills and abilities and are prepared to contribute to effective group work. If the needs of the team (such as shared goals, good operating methods, fairness, and psychological safety) are not met, then individuals are likely to argue, splinter, challenge each other, or withdraw their labor, negating any chance of achieving the task and leaving team members with a bad team experience.

Figure 1. John Adair's Team Model

This line of thought points to the seeming paradox of the group as both an entity unto itself and yet composed from the idiosyncratic styles, motives, and relationships of the individuals who comprise it. Given this paradox, Adair shows that the task, the group, *and* its individual members are all key foci for leaders.

However, all groups, no matter how well led or organized, contain tensions that can cause the group to fall apart. Teams are built from individuals with hopes, needs, desires, and fears, all of which play out in their interactions with teammates. For every team, a tension emerges between what individual members want and need for themselves and what is best for the group.

Robert Hogan notes that three basic elements of our psychological makeup—getting along, getting ahead, and making meaning—account for nearly all the wonder that is our human nature.[16] One can think of these elements as three master motives, the influence of which differs for different individuals.

The first fundamental element or motive, namely, "the drive to belong," underlies this book's focus on teams. Human beings are highly social; from an evolutionary perspective, they value getting along with one another.

The second element is a consequence of the first: all primate groups, and many non-primate ones, have status hierarchies or a pecking order. Higher-status individuals typically lead more comfortable lives than those of lower status. Although getting along with others is critical for individual survival, obtaining status in the group—getting ahead—delivers better food, fancier lodging, and more opportunities for sex. For example, high-status hunters among the Yanomamo tribes of the Amazon River Basin have two to three times as many offspring as do lower-status tribesmen.

Of course, people vary in the degree to which they choose to compete for status. For example, when a powerful executive walks into a room of ordinary staffers, most will turn their heads to look. A few will gravitate towards the executive, shake hands, stand near her, and/or engage in conversation. Others will move away, becoming shy in the presence of power. Regardless of the response chosen, each behavior is a signal to others in the room and to the executive. Approaching can be seen as a display of fawning or seeking favor. Dogs greet the alpha by cringing, licking the alpha's muzzle, and whining; humans do it by smiling, stepping close, and deferring to the alpha's preferences. Compared to their less ambitious counterparts, ambitious people will more quickly share opinions, report favorably about their own accomplishments, and solicit increased time around the alpha. This behavior sends a message to everyone else in the room: "Look at me, hanging with the big dog!" Furthermore, the behavior affords the little dog an opportunity to send the big dog a message: "Did you notice me? How about helping me move up the ladder?"

The third element incorporates some form of symbolic belief system, like a religion, which is found in all human societies. Cultural systems, values, or symbols provide a sense of meaning in life and a sense of control over seemingly random and unpredictable events. Not only do these belief systems reinforce group living through fostering a strong shared identity, but they also protected early societies by codifying anti-contagion strategies. Advocating cleanliness or forbidding the eating of swine exemplified these strategies.

For example, the declining Roman Empire had weak traditions of mutual aid; the poor and sick of Rome either cared for themselves or were left on the street to die. In contrast, the new Christian faith created norms of community, charity, and mutual aid, or, in Hogan terms, the meaning of life for Christians was to help everyone get along. Christian teachings commanded assistance to the less fortunate and promised a life beyond Earth for those who were ill. Historians suspect that many Romans converted to Christianity because the Christian community delivered a better quality of life and a greater chance of survival in times when illness meant death.[17] In the 300 years after the death of Christ, the number of Christians increased from a tiny number to around 20 million, an appreciable proportion of the human beings alive at the time.

The important point is that the first two motives bequeath to each relationship a conflict: human interaction involves a negotiation between getting along with each other and getting ahead. In teams, these relationship tensions are always present and can cause friction and fracture if not managed.

Of course, people differ in terms of getting along and getting ahead; this simple distinction is vital to understanding and predicting behavior. Some people are happy to go along and don't care about getting ahead, while others are deeply interested in being at the top of the ladder.

The American showman, businessman, and now president, Donald Trump, is a salient example of being desperate to climb to the top of the ladder. Numerous articles have said that Trump didn't risk his own money in projects like his Atlantic City casinos; instead, he charged for the use of his name and earned fees through management contracts.[18] A man who is charismatic, intimidating, and immune to criticism stripped cash from the operations for himself and then demanded that his bankers and creditors permit him to incur more debt to keep the casinos running. Although he promised to stay within credit limits when he appeared in front of bankruptcy courts, he broke the covenant within days. Even though he proved incompetent at the casino business, he was a master at persuading other people to give him money. Additionally, in his mind, the wreckage he left behind was always someone else's fault. In summary, Mr. Trump appears to be a) powerfully motivated to get ahead; b) minimally concerned about getting along with others unless it suits his primary drive; and c) tolerated by people close to him, insofar as his behavior benefits their own agendas.

Of course, most individuals aren't Mr. Trump. As an alternative, Lionel Messi, a famous footballer, is frequently described as the best player ever. Messi displays preternatural skill and footwork, and is a prolific point scorer for the Barcelona club. He is also seen as the heart of the team. He maintains positive relationships with players, coaches, and even his old youth club colleagues in Argentina. Aside from his remarkable football skill, other players acknowledge him as a warm and humble person, who always plays for the team, not his personal glory.

Teams must strike a balance between individuals' needs and group needs. What the people on a team are like matters enormously to how effectively the team will come together; the aggregate personality or group style will determine how the team approaches its tasks and goes about its work.

To grasp the dynamics of groups requires knowledge of individual personalities and group roles. In addition, coaching and driving more effective teamwork necessitates understanding the psychological dynamics of groups. More on that below.

ANCIENT LESSONS

So, what lessons for modern teaming can we derive from our brief tour through human prehistory and its psychological legacy?

The instincts for teaming can be broadly divided into two big lessons. The first is about *hard,* tangible drivers of team functioning. Teams exist for a purpose. They form around tasks or activities that cannot be carried out efficiently by one person alone. If a task doesn't call for cooperation, then it isn't necessary to form a team.

The team's purpose implies the members must achieve shared intentionality. Shared intentionality requires a mission, goal, plan, or common process in which team members understand their individual parts. Frequently, it is leaders who supply the focus, energy, and command needed to galvanize a group to act. Moreover, the team is more likely to be successful if its members are competent, meaning that they have the skills needed to accomplish the task.

> Post-industrial society makes teamwork harder than it needs to be.

Second, all groups require their members to pull together and bond, which we can describe as the *soft* aspects of teaming. Good collaboration requires a shared group identity and a willingness to subsume one's own needs for the team's needs for as long as required to achieve an outcome. It also requires that the team manage the tensions inherent in all human interactions. Since people's personalities and motivations differ, leaders and their groups must manage the tensions that emerge from these differences, or they will end up in a jumble of emotional argument, tension, and underperformance.

Getting teams to perform well can be challenging. It requires that leaders and teams understand human nature and pay attention to both the hard and soft aspects of how teams operate. The lessons of hard and soft, derived from our most basic psychology, will provide a clear focus for action.

Although teams are the natural unit for humans to get tasks done, Western post-industrial society makes teamwork harder than it needs to be. In my view, the West spent the two hundred years or so since the start of the Industrial Revolution engineering teamwork out of work life. Industrialization and large-scale manufacturing corroded our basic human instincts, and instead taught managers and workers to avoid using teams. But nature wins in the end, and with good reason teams are now making a comeback.

THE FALL AND RISE OF TEAMS

Generally speaking, would you say that most people can be trusted or that you can't be too careful in dealing with people?
— *Hogan Personality Inventory survey item*

HOW WE ENGINEERED OURSELVES OUT OF TEAMS

Today's management fashions look to technology companies as harbingers of modern, daring, and innovative management practices. More than any other company, Google has been a boon to business professors and newspapers, generating as many headlines for its unusual and indulgent working environments as for its extraordinary profits and technology. At Google, you can get a massage, take a nap in a sleep pod, access a Michelin-starred chef to prepare your free lunch, get free dry cleaning, and come to work via free transportation.

Some time ago when Google undertook basic research into the characteristics of good managers and supervisors, it overlooked teams. Although leaders certainly are important, they tend towards irrelevance without anyone to lead.[19] In fact, the best way to measure the effectiveness of a leader is to judge their teams' successes or failures. Google had 6,000 managers in a total workforce of about 40,000—the rest of the work was done in teams. Google began a two-year research project to uncover the secrets of high-performing teams, a topic we will explore in a later chapter. The larger point concerning Google's investigation is about the zeitgeist: if the internet behemoth decides teams are important, then teams are back.

This rediscovery of the importance of teams is a change from the recent industrial past, when individual efficiency mattered most and workers were often regarded as necessary nuisances rather than as thinking, creative, or even useful resources. After almost 200 years of being engineered out of existence by experts and business owners, teams only recently began reappearing as a planned feature of organizational life.

At the start of the 20th century, for example, Henry Ford, inventor of the Model T and founder of the eponymous car giant, pioneered the mass production process and consequently became a fabulously wealthy tycoon. Ford found the notion of teamwork and worker autonomy odd: "The average worker," he opined, "above all wants a job in which he does not have to think."[20] Ford's knowledge of what his workers wanted probably didn't come from asking them, so we are left to conclude that his opinion was wishful thinking.

Ford applied modern thinking to one of the emerging technologies of his age. Machinery and mechanization were the marvels of the mid-19th century, and they became a metaphor for thinking about the social organization of work, as well. Workers were adjuncts to industrial processes, akin to cogs in a bigger machine, the metaphor Charlie Chaplin satirized in his 1936 movie, *Modern Times*. In the movie, the worker (Chaplin) works in a state-of-the-art factory where the inescapable machinery dominates and subjugates him.

> The best way to measure the effectiveness of a leader is to judge their team's successes or failures.

Working in small, cohesive groups to accomplish tasks had been the norm for thousands of years prior to mass mechanization, with products done in the craft guilds and small, family-run enterprises. The Industrial Revolution, one of the most jarring and transformative events in world history, upended this approach through the use of machines that replaced workers. The colossal gains in productivity achieved through mechanization provided an enormous lift in the health, living conditions, and wealth of England, Western Europe, and the United States. The gross domestic product of Western countries soared, incomes rose, and life expectancy increased even as the population grew. Health and wealth increased so dramatically that when economic historians compare Western growth to that of India and China, they call it the Great Divergence.

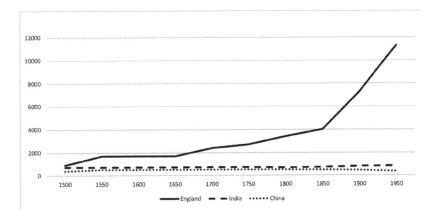

Figure 2. The Great Divergence: The Industrial Revolution and GDP Growth

These changes lifted millions of people out of poverty. However, although working conditions changed, they did not change for the better. Innovative mechanization of labor-intensive tasks produced cataclysmic effects that transformed the world. In England, for example, rural regions emptied of farm workers, due to the American invention of the mechanized grain reaper by Cyrus McCormick. His innovation liberated the wheat production potential of the enormous lands of the US Midwest, which produced so much surplus that the US began to export it, causing global wheat prices to plummet. These falling prices devastated English production, which relied on manual labor and couldn't compete with the tide of imported American grain. Country folk across England began to leave the land and their rural lives in search of work and higher wages. They flocked to the grimy cities and the new towns sprouting around the factories, mines, and mills. Automation, the wonder of the age, supplanted artisans and cottage industries and proffered instead industrial mills with long working hours, noisy, unsafe conditions and child labor. Lengthy working weeks were the norm: the word "weekend" wasn't commonly used until the 20th century.

By 1900, most working people were no longer economically independent; they relied for their livelihoods on massive industrial firms whose owners hired and fired at will. The human tide from the countryside flooded and overflowed the slums and tenements in the great cities of London and New York and across Europe. If they were lucky, workers lived regimented lives in model villages built next to factories by paternalistic dynasties like the Cadburys in England or Kelloggs in America. If they were unlucky, they lived twenty to a room in a rat-infested warren in the Lower East Side of New York.

The use of machinery and automation caused work to become more individualized and less group-based. Reflecting the spirit of the age, the Scientific Management movement, introduced by the American Frederick Taylor, sought to apply industrial-machine logic to human workers and work processes. Taylor's work-design principles emphasized dividing jobs into narrow activities with strict behavioral prescriptions derived from measuring the most productive workers. Arranged and ordered in exacting detail, tasks were completed in short, repetitive work cycles.

Henry Ford was an enthusiastic Taylor devotee and led the way with the mass industrialization of car manufacturing. Workers were conceptualized as interchangeable hands, paid only to complete single tasks along a production line.

The apogee of this trend can be found in Ford's observation that, of the 7,882 manual procedures required to assemble his famous Model T automobile, 2,637 could be done by one-legged men; 670 by legless men; 715 by one-armed men; and 2 by armless men.[21] Given that Ford was not an early adopter of programs to employ the disabled, we can only wonder if he had considered what a headless man might accomplish. Actually, history has noted that Ford did indeed wonder if the worker's cranium could be dispensed with: "Why is it that when I ask for a pair of hands, a brain comes attached?"

Western (i.e., mostly American) folklore and icons underpin the centuries-long trend of the atomization of work. This culture celebrates prodigies struggling in seclusion to produce scientific, artistic, financial, or musical masterpieces. Talented sporting stars get kudos for team performances, and in business the mythology of the lone leader is familiar to all. But Jack Welch didn't single-handedly rebuild GE, and Mark Zuckerberg had a team around him to birth the wonder that is Facebook. The canon of leadership and management thinking has unhappily focused the vast majority of its attention on anomalous individuals rather than on productive groups.

The cult of the individual, despite its intuitive appeal, fails as an explanation for the development of business, science, medicine, architecture, military know-how, or the discovery of new lands. Michelangelo painted the Sistine Chapel with a team of 16 other painters. The Romans didn't conquer Carthage or Gaul because they were *individually* better fighters than the natives; rather, the key to the Romans' success was their talent for military and social coordination. Once the conquered tribes learned the habits of coordinated action taught by their Roman overlords, the tribes promptly overran the Roman leaders who were waging war against each other.

All significant human accomplishments—from discovering agriculture, to constructing the pyramids and the Great Wall of China, to building innumerable cathedrals, roads, cities and modern organizations—are the result of group effort, of collective and highly coordinated enterprise.

THE REBIRTH OF TEAMS

The pendulum, however, has begun to swing back, and the era of tightly controlled, individualistic work has begun to fade. The decline of manufacturing, globalization, technology, and knowledge work all mitigate for teamwork. Deloitte's 2016 survey found that:

> [A] new organizational model is on the rise: a "network of teams" in which companies build and empower teams to work on specific business projects and challenges. These networks are aligned and coordinated with operations and information centers similar to command centers in the military. Indeed, in some ways, businesses are becoming more like Hollywood movie production teams and less like traditional corporations, with people coming together to tackle projects, then disbanding and moving on to new assignments once the project is complete.[22]

Surveys of the *Fortune* 1000 largest US firms have reported that, although in 1987, 28% of employees worked in firms that used teams, the percentage expanded to 68% by 1995 and is set between 50 and 70% in most workplaces today.[23] Products, markets, and customers change quickly, even in the most traditional industries. Now it has become more efficient for groups of workers to decide for themselves how they should structure their work, instead of passing decisions up and down the hierarchy and finally into the hands of a manager who can reorganize the group's priorities.[24]

Toyota and the modern quality movement is a great example. After WWII, the Japanese developed a passion for the ideas of an American quality guru, W. Edwards Deming. Toyota's automotive division took his ideas to the factory floor and began feeding data to work teams about their productivity and the quality of their work. The teams were able to review their work processes from start to finish. They had the power to establish tradeoffs between productivity and quality, to suggest changes to production techniques, to generate efficiencies, and to offer ideas for other improvements. Deming was a distant, tough statistician, but the Japanese revered him. When asked at a dinner whether he had learned anything from the workers, he said, "People are important."[25]

Teams have become more popular because mechanization is giving way to knowledge work, and data-intense firms have realized that people dislike operating like cogs in a machine. Allowing work groups to think about and organize their own activities reduces the need for layers of hierarchy. The experiments in large organizations, undertaken mostly by the Japanese, Germans, Danes, and Swedes through the 1970s and 1980s have been gradually adopted worldwide. Rather than define the minimum of what is required ("pick up envelope, place form in envelope, lick strip, close, place on complete pile"), employers are asking much more from their employees ("Can you think of how to improve this process?"). This change has had a positive impact on workers. Employees perform better, behave more ethically, and appear more pleased with their work lives.

Today, dozens of variants of teams are appearing at work. Project teams, quality teams, self-organizing teams, agile teams, lean teams, virtual teams, cross-functional teams, leaderless teams, even executive teams. The trend is unlikely to slow down.

At the end of the 20th century, Western countries exported labor-intensive work to developing countries, and in the opening decades of the 21st century, those countries started replacing labor with technology. Consequently, the amount of manual work has diminished globally. In contrast, the percentage of knowledge work and service work has grown dramatically across the world. Although such work is difficult to Taylorize, it's well-suited to collaboration.

Software development is a good example of collaborative work. Google and Facebook are poster children for decentralized, networked organizations, in which teams come together for a project, then disperse, then reconvene with new members and specialists for another project. Hot-desking, in which individuals are expected to share workspaces on a temporary basis, is the norm. Advertising agencies, telecommunications firms, large consultancies, and even bureaucratic government agencies have shifted to organizing work around specific tasks or outputs in place of creating permanent divisions.

The military, which has always organized itself around groups, is exhibiting a renewed interest in using teams as an antidote to their staggeringly inefficient bureaucracies. The military guru advocating this change, General Stanley McChrystal, who led American special forces in Afghanistan, wondered why the large, well-trained, superbly equipped American force was losing to Al Qaeda when Al Qaeda had to scramble to recruit locals and smuggle in foreign fighters. His answer was the American bureaucratic over-engineering baked into managerial thought and practice. The bureaucracy produced competing electronic systems, mixed objectives, and personal turf wars between different commands.

Similarly, McChrystal observed Al Qaeda's success lay in the operational flexibility it afforded combat units and the strong connections it fostered between them: "We just needed to reshape the superstructure that bound those [US] teams together to look more like the bonds within those [Al Qaeda] teams. We dubbed this approach 'Team of Teams.'"[26]

His response was to decentralize authority by creating autonomous teams who could make fast operational decisions, using real-time information about war activities that was passed to everyone from a central data source. McChrystal achieved a dramatic increase in operational tempo and effectiveness: over four years, his force went from 15 to 300 operations a month, with minimal increases in manpower and resources. More dramatically, he built the new system in five weeks.

McChrystal didn't alter the formal structure of the military, which should be an object lesson to CEOs too prepared to reach for the "restructure" trigger. Instead, he instituted the ancient lessons we saw earlier: a clear mission understood by all, shared information, and trusted commanders who made their own operational decisions.

If a team strategy worked for the military, wouldn't it work for organizations? Smart firms are increasingly attracted to teams for four reasons: first and foremost, teams increase employee engagement and provide a natural way of working. Shared goals unite and promote a special identity that people enjoy. Engagement grows when people feel connected to their work, their firm, and their colleagues. Moreover, research has shown that engaged employees outperform non-engaged workers and that engaged teams significantly outperform disinterested teams.[27]

Second, teams suit the changing nature of work. As work becomes less structured and extends across geographies and organizational silos, even into other firms, teams allow knowledge and skills to blend.

Third, teams offer increased organizational agility and responsiveness. Some organizations, like the online footwear retailer Zappos, have taken a radical approach to employee autonomy by allowing customer service teams to make any decision necessary to improve the experience for customers. This approach enables the firm to respond quickly to shifting trends and fashions and to maintain a deeply loyal staff.

Finally, teams provide organizations with flatter hierarchies at less expense. Nor has removing managerial control and layers of industrial bureaucracy decimated organizational perfor-

> Teams suit the changing nature of work.

mance. Toyota's experience has shown that teams intensify focus on the task at hand, resulting in significant knowledge sharing, in productivity gains, and in improved systems and processes.

For these reasons, the decline of teamwork that accompanied the mass industrialization of the last 200 years is beginning to wane. For reasons of morale, efficiency, flexibility, and cost, firms are learning to revert to a more natural way of working.

Of course, to realize these gains, teams must be well composed and well managed. The next chapter explores the hard and soft aspects of making teams work.

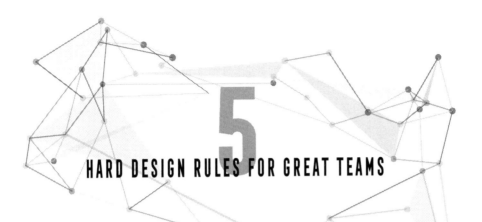

HARD DESIGN RULES FOR GREAT TEAMS

Whether it be the sweeping eagle in his flight, or the open apple blossom, the toiling workhorse, the blithe swan, the branching oak, the winding stream at its base, the drifting clouds, over all the coursing sun, form ever follows function, and this is the law.

— Louis Sullivan

The following presents a true example of exceptionally good teamwork.

Boston thoracic surgeon Atul Gawande was in the middle of a routine operation when suddenly, things went wrong. The patient's body cavity filled with blood because Gawande had accidentally cut an artery. Fortunately, the surgical crew assisting him had clear roles and were practiced, calm, and prepared. The surgeon tied off the artery as a resident extracted the blood, and a nurse whisked in four units of blood that had been stacked before the surgery began, just in case they were needed. The patient was saved.

This example is appealing because it suggests that the quiet, calm efficiency of the team's response would be the ideal for all teams. When I first began working with teams, I was enamored of the idea that harmony and an absence of conflict were the keys to effectiveness. This is an attractive idea, especially to anyone who may have worked in a hostile or combative environment. But I was dead wrong. In research that I and others have conducted since,[28] success and winning nearly always produce happier teams, but teams without conflict don't produce success, because harmony and cohesion on their own cannot deliver performance.[29]

In his books, *Complications* and *The Checklist Manifesto*, Gawande points out that good teams have a clear, shared understanding, not only of the goal, but of how to accomplish the goal.[30] He also notes that successful teams engage in considerable practice and encode their practice and knowledge in checklists and shared procedures. Top sports teams do the same. Similarly, the kitchen staff in Michelin-starred restaurants is well-rehearsed; every person understands what he or she must do to deliver the desired outcome (although there will be a lot more noise and clamor than seen in operating theatres).

The "what" and "how" are *hard* characteristics of high-performing teams. We'll explore the other tangible elements of good teamwork below.

THE TASK DETERMINES THE TEAM

The essence of all teams is a task that can't be completed by one person alone (remember the example of holding the branch down and picking the fruit). Tasks that require more than one person to deliver the desired outcome create *interdependence*. Hanging out with friends or colleagues for company doesn't require interdependence, which makes these gatherings groups, not teams.

Obviously, some tasks don't require people to work interdependently. For example, a group of people might have the same goals—a real estate sales office or a knitting circle, say—but all have individual targets and complete tasks that don't require the members to cooperate. Even if the knitting circle's performance measure is the total number of socks knitted, making the knitters share their tasks is likely to hinder the creation of socks and spawn disharmony amongst friends. If this seems obvious, rest assured it isn't, and be sure to read, below, Levi's multi-million-dollar failure to grasp this essential point. However, regardless of the task, humans still like to gather for identity and belonging; groups will form in every workplace, to foster congeniality.

In addition to an appropriate task, teamwork requires shared intentions—that is, an appreciation, not only of the task, but of how the team will work together to achieve it. As apparent as that might seem, a shared understanding of what the team needs to achieve and how it should achieve it is profoundly important to the team's success or failure. In short: clear goals *plus* cohesion *lead to* team success.[31]

Thinking about goals and focusing on the task is beneficial in designing teams and team processes.[32] Can people achieve the goal themselves, without interacting, coordinating, or sharing tasks? Or is the task a complex one that requires knowl-edge from more than one person and the work of many hands to complete?

Building a house can be done by one person—but building it is faster, safer, easi-er, and more congenial if a construction crew works together. Likewise, running a burger bar could conceivably be done by someone working alone, but if a crowd of customers comes in all at once, the customers' needs can be met better by setting up a cooking line.

On the other hand, some tasks are terrible for teams, a waste of time and coordi-nation. For example, having a group of people in a call center answer the same call, debate responses, create solutions together, and all communicate back to the customer would degrade customer service, not enhance it. The task simply doesn't require teamwork because such centers are huge rooms full of individual customer service agents.

When structuring the team or group, everything should follow its function or mis-sion. Thinking in this way leads inevitably to questions about the skills that are re-quired; the coordination necessary to support the team; and the communication, leadership, and processes that will help the team operate effectively. A simple way to think through these issues is to divide different types of teams into a grid, based on the requirement for coordination and cooperation on the one hand, and task complexity on the other.

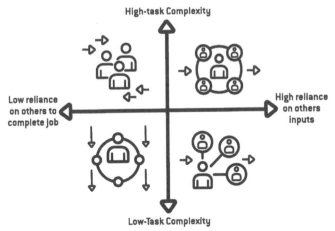

Figure 3. Patterns of Workflow Define the Team

This idea was originally mooted by Steiner in the 1960s, but remains a powerful design tool. As Figure 3 illustrates, determining if there is a need for teamwork at all, or deciding how much teamwork is necessary in any given situation, can be represented by four types of work. Task complexity controls the type of team required, whereas the level of interdependence needed to complete the task further defines the optimal team.

TYPE 4—HIGH COMPLEXITY, HIGH RELIANCE: PURE TEAM

Highly complex tasks that require considerable interaction between members and input from others are best served through teamwork. Examples include a Navy SEAL team in combat and the production crew of a live television broadcast—even, at their best, the executive team of a large corporation. Each person needs to be aware of the overall goal and the game plan; team members must be alert to each other's roles in order to respond quickly to problems or changes.

TYPE 3—HIGH COMPLEXITY, LOW RELIANCE: ORGANIZED GROUP

Sometimes groups must complete complex tasks, but only need to coordinate informally or at specific times. In such situations, the need for reliance is not great. Auditors, for example, complete complex tasks individually but check in with each other and the audit lead on the overall trends and findings. The overall report is typically the aggregated work of the group, coordinated by one or two leaders.

Some work units might work as a team for a part of the project and work individually when they don't need to coordinate. For example, video game developers intersperse periods of individual work—coding elements, building individual characters, or working on sound—and periods of coordinated activity as they construct the game, test it, and refine it.

TYPE 2—LOW COMPLEXITY, HIGH RELIANCE: SPECIALIZED TEAM

This type of team requires some coordinated action, even though the tasks are straightforward. The work can be characterized as sequential—passed from one person to another, with each worker adding a bit more to the product. Production plants in which an object is built piecemeal, as in some garment factories or in the original Model T production line, are good examples. These types of teams are becoming increasingly rare in the developed world, as robotics displaces human workers.

TYPE 1—LOW COMPLEXITY, LOW RELIANCE: SIMPLE GROUP

Completing fairly simple tasks that don't need coordinated, cooperative behavior is the least pure form of teamwork. For instance, people who work in a plant nursery, where much of the day is spent weeding, planting seedlings, lifting trays, repotting roses, and serving customers, might work alongside others. Even though they enjoy the connection and camaraderie of colleagues, the work doesn't require a high level of interaction. The group might call themselves the "seedlings team," but they aren't technically a team.

The table below summarizes the functional flow of work and how it changes the operating and leadership dynamics of the team.

TABLE 2. TEAM TYPES AND OPERATING CHARACTERISTICS

	Team type	Description	Operating style
1	Simple group	Lowest degree of coordination required; members complete their work assignments independently, and work is aggregated as the group's output.	Independent staff fulfill independent functions but work in the same place for the sake of efficiency. Staff enjoy being together and can be trained collectively, but they are managed individually.
2	Specialized team	Members perform specialized tasks. They interact with a subset of other members to complete the team's work.	Like in a software coding team, members work by themselves and also join forces to create the final product. Shared goals, common standards, and coordination are vital to success.
3	Organized group	Members interact to carry out tasks that are completed in a prearranged order; interaction only occurs between members performing tasks that are next to each other in the sequence.	Like in a production line, members depend on work flowing from one to another. Coordination and training are important, so team cohesion matters.
4	Pure team	Highest level of coordination and interaction. Members have discretion in terms of what and with whom they work, thereby exhibiting a maximal degree of shared understanding regarding mission and processes.	Like in a surgical team, members must coordinate on the fly and may sometimes step well outside their formal roles. Communication and shared situational awareness are crucial.

Teams can be extremely inefficient. Putting a team to work on a task that can reasonably be done by a single person or by a group working independently will simply add unnecessary transaction costs—meeting, coordinating, and planning.

Although people often like the feeling that comes from working together, teams should be thought of as a solution—but only to the appropriate problem. Table 2 is a diagnostic that anyone contemplating implementing a team should work through before implementation.

TEAM SIZE

Can one person be a team?
Can two people be a team?
Can twenty people be a team?

> Teams should be thought of as a solution—but only to the appropriate problem.

Professor Richard Hackman of Harvard, who was a great thinker about teams, once remarked, "My rule of thumb is no double digits. Big teams usually end up wasting everybody's time."[33]

Hackman was right. Leaders who invoke team spirit across a whole organization are well-intentioned, possibly charismatic, but by and large naïve. To refer to the whole organization as one team is a mistake. Applying knowledge about human nature can help determine the right size for a team.

Just after the turn of the new century, evolutionary psychologist Robin Dunbar completed a study of Christmas-card-sending behaviors of the English.[34] Dunbar wasn't particularly interested in Christmas, nor in Christmas cards, but he was fascinated to learn the average number of households to which cards were sent. As he expected, that number turned out to be approximately 150, a number that is close to the size of the average Facebook user's network and comparable to the size of hunter-gatherer village networks.[35] Dunbar contended that humans have a hard-coded mental limit to the number of relationships they can maintain: about 150 people, give or take. W. L. Gore, makers of Gortex fabric, limits the size of all its business divisions to roughly 150 employees, forcing divisions to split if they grow larger. Dunbar's theory is that once a network grows larger than 150, the number of connections becomes too difficult to handle effectively.

As for teams, Dunbar thinks that the right number is no larger than 15 (the size of a rugby team) and that the ideal number is fewer. For example, the Roman Army was organized around small groups of eight to 10 soldiers; each group joined with nine others to form a century of 100 soldiers. As Dunbar points out:

> . . . All modern armies are structured along these lines, so this sort of layer of 150 general friends that you have, turns out to consist of a series of layers which are scaled very tightly with respect to each other: each layer is three times bigger than the other; so you have an inner, inner core of intimate friends and relations, of about five, and then there's the next layer out, it's about 15. If you like to think of those as best friends, perhaps, they're the people you might do most of your social Saturday evening barbeques with, and that of course, includes the five inside. And then this next layer out is 50 (you might think of those as good friends), and the 150, your friends. And then we know there are at least two more layers beyond that: one at 500 which you might think of as acquaintances, so again this is including everybody within the 150 as well; finally, one at 1500, who are basically the number of faces you can put names to. But you see those numbers absolutely replicated beautifully across modern armies: that's how they're all structured, and they just carry on with the next series out, so 5000, 15000, 50000.[36]

Jeff Bezos, the well-known CEO of Amazon (which now takes 53 cents of every dollar spent online), also thinks that bigger is not better, at least with regard to teams. As a result, he has enshrined his "two-pizza rule." Bezos observed that the larger the meeting, the less the participation and the greater the group-think. Any more people than can be fed from two pizzas is probably too many at a meeting or in a team. He instituted this rule across Amazon, requesting that meetings and teams be kept to the number of employees that two pizzas can feed.

> The larger the meeting, the less the participation and the greater the group-think.

Science supports the two-pizza rule. As the number of people in a team increases, the number of connections rises exponentially. That is, a team constituting five people presents 10 links to manage or maintain. When there are 10 people on the team, that number balloons to 45! The formula for mapping this increase is:

$$\frac{n\,(n-1)}{2}$$

n=number of people on the team.

As shown in Figure 4, by the time a team consists of 15 people, the number of possible connections is over 100.

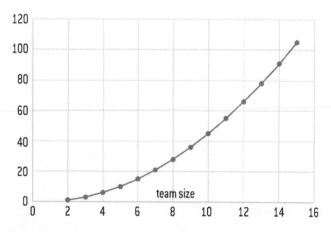

Figure 4: Connections Grow Exponentially

It's tempting to believe that boosting a team's size creates the potential for increased specialization and expanded knowledge. The evidence clearly shows the opposite, and a team's actual productivity suffers. Increasing a team's size makes its coordination more difficult, diminishes member motivation, and increases conflict.[37]

A study of a large hospital's emergency department demonstrates why small teams produce better outcomes than do large teams. A large group of more than 30 doctors and nurses was divided into six-person pods, each led by a senior doctor.[38] As one nurse remarked, "[Before the pods were established], you had to walk across the ED all timid and get up a bit of courage and say to a doctor, 'Uh, excuse me?'" In smaller teams, workmates began to claim each other rather than blame each other:

> Now there is much more of a sense of ownership of each other. I'll say, "My pod isn't running well. Where is my doctor?" and he'll be accountable to me. And the doctors will say, "Where are my nurses, who do I have today?" whereas it used to be, "Who is this patient's nurse?" ignoring that the nurse had any relationship to the doctor.

In addition, the pods lead to efficiency gains. Tracking 160,000 patients served by the department during the six months before the pods and 12 months after the pods were created revealed improved efficiencies. For example, patients' throughput time, the time from patient arrival to time of discharge, fell from eight hours to five and a half hours per patient, a 40% decrease in the amount of time a patient spent being treated. Furthermore, this improvement was accomplished without increasing staffing levels.

So, Hackman was probably right: if a group comprises many more than 10 members, it will soon begin to devolve into subgroups. Humans much prefer small working groups, although, as armies have shown throughout human history, small, *well-run* units can combine into mighty forces.

TRACKING PROGRESS

Anyone who spends time with a professional sports team can't help but be amazed by the sheer volume and detail of data that is captured about every possible performance variable. For the All Blacks rugby team, a very partial list includes: body mass, stature, weight, weight gain, muscle mass, VO2, deadweight lift, skinfold thickness, body fat, fastest 10m sprint, fastest 20m sprint, tackle count, tries scored, meters covered, tackles missed, passes dropped, attack 1st 3, defense 1st 3, turnovers, evasion, line breaks, and on and on. Equally as impressive is how seriously everyone takes the data—players, coaches, support staff, and management. Players and coaches review plays endlessly, to glean a competitive advantage. They give each other feedback and track changes and improvements obsessively. And that's just their own performance—never mind the time spent analyzing the opposition's data.

Take the time to think of your own team. What individual and group performance variables are captured? How frequently do they get reviewed? How specific are the improvement targets you have for your own performance? For the team?

People are surprised if the same process is used with teams at work, often voicing responses like, "We can't do that, we've got work to do." or "Oh, that's a bit over the top. We all know what we are doing."

Actually, it's not over the top. It's called professionalism.

A behavioral technology that emerged from Japan in 1986 shows how the same approach can revolutionize work teams. In the 1980s, Japanese industry was the wonder of the world—inventive, lean, and high quality. Japan had been heavily influenced by W. Edwards Deming, the efficiency expert who had transformed Toyota. He combined rigorous statistical control techniques with a movement to put decision-making power in the hands of workers to transform production. Teams worked better when given objectives, not tasks.[39] The best teams were those who received broad goals with the autonomy to devise their own tactics to achieve the objective. The subtitle of the *Harvard Business Review* paper describing the approach was, "Stop running the relay race and take up rugby."

Rugby of course, is an analogy to emphasize the interdependent nature of winning a game. One of the most useful team technologies to emerge from this line of management thinking is called "Scrum," which derives, delightfully, from rugby. In rugby, a scrum is an ordered formation between the opposing forwards, during which they grapple and strive against each other. Scrum refers today to a set of techniques to keep a team focused on the objective and aware of every member's contribution. When done well, Scrum creates a visible, transparent view of the team's goal, by charting progress, issues, bottlenecks, wins, and backlogs. The following quote describes a daily stand-up or Scrum meeting for a software development team:

> The Daily Scrum is a meeting for coordinating the work of the developer team, which happens once a day. To keep the meeting short, each developer answers only the following three questions:
>
> 1. What have you done since yesterday?
> 2. What do you plan to do today?
> 3. What impediments are in the way?

During the Daily Scrum meeting, developers are not allowed to talk about issues with their cat, show demos of their latest work, or tell heroic stories of programming problems solved: the focus is on the big picture and how the team is tracking.[40]

In implementing a half-billion-dollar road construction project, my consulting group used a version of the Scrum technique. We installed huge signage boards across the whole site, to show individual work-crews an overall picture of what they were constructing. We visually tracked progress across the whole site via images, measures, and celebrations of milestones. Working towards something tangible, and seeing the movement towards it, is far more motivating than laboring without any visuals to mark progress.

I'm not suggesting that Scrum will suit every team. I *am* suggesting that teams who present performance data and feedback to the whole team and openly discuss that data will be well on the road to improving and winning.

THE LESSONS OF THE HARD

In the late 1990s, Levi Strauss & Co. began a misguided experiment in teamwork.[41] Traditionally, Levi's jeans were made using a piecework system. Workers operated in an assembly line and were paid according to their individual productivity. Levi organized workers into work units of between 10 and 35 people; each unit would share its tasks and be paid according to the total number of

> The more senior the team, the less care or thought is dedicated to its performance.

jeans produced (*a change to the hard*). Management thought this change created a more benevolent system that would reduce stress, pressure, and the monotony of piecework.

What they thought was going to be a successful solution led instead to a human relations and production disaster. Skilled workers now found that their rewards were dependent on the performance of the slowest member of the team, and that they had no way to make the group work faster. Corrosive infighting, threats, and insults became common, and longtime friendships dissolved as faster workers tried to banish slower ones. Labor costs and the unit cost of a pair of jeans increased. Levi abandoned the experiment and shifted production offshore. The trial ultimately came at the expense of hurt lives, closed plants, lost production, and millions of dollars.

Most teams simply begin working with no real design or planning. They get underway with minimal thought or effort; they throw themselves into activity without taking the time to follow a structured approach. When I've worked with teams in the past, I called this behavior "flight to task." Having worked with over 50 executive teams, my observation has been that the more senior the team, the less care or thought is dedicated to its performance. I don't think this is because they are intentionally sloppy or careless. Rather they make an assumption that teamwork occurs as a matter of course, and they treat it as an unconscious process that adds nothing to their work. In this they are well-intentioned but naïve. Were they instead to treat their performance in the same way elite sports franchises do, what level of performance might they reach?

Good science[42] supports the importance of the hard side of teams. Recommendations include making the team mission visible, clarifying behavior expectations, getting the right number of competent and socially adept people on board, and ensuring that team members have the resources and buy-in to win. Once a team meets these criteria, it should succeed—unless members are seduced by their own success or fail to manage the social dynamics required to work together effectively.

6
THE LESSONS OF THE SOFT

No member of a crew is praised for the rugged individuality of his rowing.
Ralph Waldo Emerson

Many businessmen tend to dismiss the soft elements of high-performing teams as irrelevant or too touchy-feely, but these elements are neither trivial nor irrelevant. Such disregard stems partly from a macho overconfidence and partly from the team-development industry's capture by trendy, human-potential disciples who are devoted to running team-building games as an end in themselves. Many team leaders and managers recall with distaste their own experiences of trust falls, forced intimacy, heroic drinking sessions, and irrelevant motivational slogans.

But the soft elements of team performance reflect a kind of social technology, or interpersonal software, that enables and supports our ultra-sociality. Don't forget that, historically, warfare and defending territory and resources were key drivers of teamwork, and that social technologies evolved to help teams cohere, commit, and coordinate in order to win. These elements are as important as the more visible hard factors we explored in the last chapter. Five soft features impact team dynamics and performance: fairness, cohesion, trust, communication, and conflict.

FAIRNESS

Because we evolved as cooperative beings who nonetheless engaged in frequent between-group conflict, modern competitive sports offer a useful way of exploring teamwork. This is for three reasons: first, team member cooperation and coordination are highly visible; second, success and failure are obvious; and third, sports teamwork reveals the micro-level interactions that constitute the softer side of teams.

Consider, for example, the vast sums that are spent on recruiting highly skilled and talented players: Manchester United, an English football team (or soccer in the US), spent over £1 billion on wages in the five years leading up to 2015, and for good reason, as high wages correlate with top-five finishes.

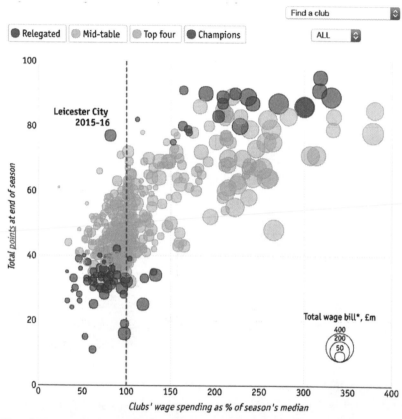

Figure 5. Wages and Performance in Football http://infographics.economist.com/2016/football_scatter/

The miraculous success of the Leicester Foxes winning the English Premier football league in 2016, or the Iceland national football team, all amateurs, making the Euro 2016 quarterfinals, is just that—miraculous. However, while the notion that more talent equals better performance is broadly true, it certainly does not tell the whole story. Expensive star talent matters, of course, but the number of star players isn't necessarily the deciding factor in ultimate success.

To explore this point, two economists studied the salary differentials of major league baseball teams in the United States.[43] For teams in which a single star player earns many times the salaries paid to his or her teammates, performance deteriorates; in other words, beyond a certain point, inequality proves detrimental to teamwork.

In addition, the two economists discovered that baseball salary inequality has increased over time:

TABLE 3. MAJOR LEAGUE BASEBALL SALARY INEQUALITY

PERCENTILE	1985 CUMULATIVE SALARY	2002 CUMULATIVE SALARY
Highest 10% of players	25%	40%
Second highest 10%	17	23
Third highest 10%	14	14
Lowest 70%	44	23

At the time of writing this book, Clayton Kershaw of the Los Angeles Dodgers earned $32.8 million; the average starting salary for a newly signed player is $515,000, and the league average salary is $4 million. Before discussing why inequality should concern all team leaders, asking *why* the wage gap is growing is a worthwhile exercise. The answer has little to do with science and a great deal to do with male, ultra-rich, ego-driven team owners. Successful and wealthy, the owners compete with each other to display their affluence through trophy-player acquisitions, in the belief that highly paid stars will transform the season and win every contest. This practice inflates the value of stars, often at the expense of the amount left for other players. Such competition is akin to an arms race: teams that are better endowed financially drive team owners who cannot compete to the ranks of the also-rans. But with sports that require a great deal of interdependence, buying stars is *not* the path to the success that it first seems.

The economists divided the baseball teams into quartiles, based on the inequality of wages among the players. Between 1992 and 2001, teams with the smallest levels of salary inequality won an average of eight games *more* than did teams with the greatest salary inequality. Subsequent investigations have confirmed this trend, at least with baseball teams.[44] Even though success tends to follow the total salary spent (the higher the team salaries, the greater their success), acquiring a megastar and expecting that he or she will transform a team's season is not a sure path to winning the league championship.

> More talent is not
> necessarily better.

In other sports, the notion that more talent is necessarily better also fails to hold true, particularly when the sport requires considerable team coordination and cooperation. That is, when *task interdependence* is high, team members must coordinate their behavior to compete successfully. Compared to other sports, baseball tends to require less interdependence because the pitcher's ability is often considered the main ingredient in winning or losing games.

In contrast, task interdependence is much higher in basketball and in both US football and soccer (non-US football); in these sports, team performance is not simply the sum of the players' individual talents and skills. On one hand, the whole may perform better than the sum of its parts; on the other hand, status competition *inside* teams can lead individuals to focus their attention on fighting for intra-group rank, rather than directing their efforts toward coordination and team performance.

In 2010, the Miami Heat basketball team managed to sign two of the top players in the NBA—LeBron James and Chris Bosh. With this superstar lineup, the Heat was expected to become the modern version of the Chicago Bulls, a powerhouse champion team, but they performed *worse* than they had the year before, without the stars. In high-interdependence teams, more talent does not equal better performance. The key point is that the complex mix of relationships, cohesion, and fit matters at least as much as raw talent.

One study explicitly tested the idea that performance is not a simple matter of attracting stars.[45] Comparing performance in baseball, football, and basketball, Adam Galinsky and Robert Swaab found that stars help lift team performance in high-interdependence sports in which players can interact dozens of times with each other to make one play. But stars only enhance performance up to a certain point; after that point is reached, players begin to compete for status within the team and team performance falls away:

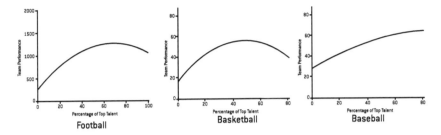

Figure 6: Stars and Performance

Galinsky called this the "too much talent effect," and the lesson is clear. Teams who work with exceptionally skilled and talented people are willing to see such individuals rewarded differently—but only up to a point. If a team includes LeBron James, team members understand that his talent and skill merit higher pay. However, if the star's fame overshadows the team's, and if his pay seems unfair, then trouble is likely to result. In conclusion, the most efficient strategy for an owner to follow is to build a team of competent performers, all of whom are paid approximately the same amount, and invest the savings in coaching, training, and developing teamwork to produce above-average performances.

That raw talent is not an unequivocal good is illustrated by the story of Terrell Owens, an individually gifted player in the American NFL. Although teams competed to sign him, they soon discovered that he was a net cost for the team. He played for the San Francisco 49ers, the Philadelphia Eagles, the Dallas Cowboys, the Buffalo Bills, the Cincinnati Bengals, and finally, the Allen Wranglers. Across these assignments, Owens accrued a reputation for sabotaging teams and destroying morale. He never accepted responsibility for his errors, blaming others instead. He fought with his own teammates and undermined their confidence with mocking, sarcastic remarks. He failed to show up to practice and argued with his coaches. Many coaches believed that in a new team culture, he would respond in positive ways. Or that if they gave him a position of authority (i.e., a leadership role), he would mature and adopt a new persona. But this change never occurred. Owens ended his career by being passed from team to team, leaving unhappy managers and teammates in his wake. The moral of the story is that talent comes packaged with individual differences in temperament, character, and values, and all of which will impact the team.

A final example of trust and fairness comprises the pirates of the 18th and 19th centuries. To be in line for a share of the rewards, the entire crew shared in the risks and hazards of combat, or else they were dealt with. Offering them the chance to be first into battle tested the shirkers and freeloaders. If they failed the test, they were tried and made to walk the plank. Most pirate crews had a formal written constitution that specified the laws and the punishments for breaking them; it also explicitly outlined the structure of sharing in rewards—maybe not equally, but fairly.[46] After deducting costs and conferring awards for injury (for example, the loss of a right arm was worth approximately 500 pieces of eight; an eye was worth 100 pieces of eight or one slave), the pirates would receive their just rewards. Leeson describes the process of dividing up the spoils as follows:

> These amounts being withdrawn from the capital, the rest of the Prize would be divided in as many portions as men on the ship. The Captain draws four or five men's portions for the use of the ship, perhaps even more, and draws two portions for himself. The rest of the men share uniformly, and the boys get a half a man's share. When a ship is robbed, nobody must plunder and keep his loot to himself. Everything taken— money, jewels, precious stones and goods—must be shared among them all, without any man enjoying a penny more than his fair share.[47]

If even pirates wouldn't tolerate freeloaders or loafers, why should modern teams?

It's a great question, and one that lies at the heart of team politics. The answer lies in the psychological dilemmas built into the heart of humans' moral reaction to freeloaders. We all want to belong—to retain cohesion with our fellow travelers and at the same time maximize rewards for ourselves. That means that people can tolerate a lack of contribution and will even tolerate incompetent fools over unpleasant jerks to retain cohesion.[48] But groups won't tolerate helping oneself to the rewards while not contributing a fair effort to the task. Modern-day corporate pirates, like hedge-fund entrepreneurs, would do well to understand that point.

COHESION

What is it that binds a team together and creates camaraderie? It's a combination of shared intentionality (task cohesion) and mutual support (social cohesion) within the team.

The following example illustrates how cohesion affects team performance.

In 1913, a French engineer called Maximilien Ringelmann conducted a series of tests. He told teams of men to haul a load on a rope. He found that as the size of the team increased, the effort exerted by individual pullers *decreased* so that, in a team of 10, team members didn't pull as much as they did in a team of four. Ringelmann thought this strange result (now called the Ringelmann effect) was caused by coordination problems, but he was wrong. Instead, the effect relies on an important element of our psychology: the tendency to experience less cohesion and exert less effort as group size increases. The term psychologists use for this phenomenon is "social loafing."

The effects of social loafing have been observed in a plethora of collective human endeavors. For example, the impact of the phenomenon was well demonstrated in experiments that asked people to shout as loud as they could by themselves.[49] The experimenter recorded the volume in decibels, then paired the individual with another study participant; both participants wore earmuffs so that they couldn't judge each other's volume. The result was that individuals reduced their volume by about 30% when they were shouting as a pair. In groups of six, the volume each person generated fell by nearly 70%. Just knowing someone else was nearby led to a reduction of effort. In addition, social loafing was implicated as a factor in the infamous downing of a US helicopter by two US Air Force jets in Iraq. The review of the incident concluded that the responsibility was "spread so thin by the laws of social impact and by confused authority relationships that no one felt compelled to act."[50]

The explanation for social loafing is worth pursuing. First, each individual's contribution can be hidden in the group's collective effort, so freeloaders have an opportunity to cruise at the expense of others instead of making an intense personal effort. Second, as shown in the shouting experiment, if people cannot judge how much effort someone else is making, how can they know if they are doing their fair share? Another quirk of human nature is that people tend to overestimate their contributions; although their performance may have degraded, they continue to feel like they are contributing more. Third, if the task itself has no real meaning for the individuals involved, they won't exert the effort that they would exhibit if the task were relevant, personal, and urgent, as occurred when the Farmy Army turned out to help Christchurch in the aftermath of the huge earthquake.

Finally, team research has documented a link between group size, low cohesion, and social loafing. In a field study that investigated 23 teams, the findings indicated that the larger the group and the less connected its members felt, the more social loafing occurred. Large groups that lack cohesion perform less effectively than smaller groups who feel connected.

There are four key counters to social loafing, each of which can boost team efficacy by increasing the likelihood that individual team members will apply maximum effort.[51] The first is that transparency of effort (i.e., publicly documenting each member's performance) deters loafing. In an interesting application of this phenomenon, the Cambridge University Boat Club posted objective performance results in the gym and, next to it, a sheet with subjective assessments by the coaches.[52] The assessments explained what each person had and had not done well and provided explicit guidance on what each person should do to improve. Even though this transparency might discomfit some of the team members, it highlighted any instances of social loafing, and drove intense competition not to seem to be shirking.

As an aside, research has revealed that spectators are adept at detecting team cohesion, and that their cohesion judgments predict a team's winning percentage surprisingly well. By showing judges only 10-second samples of ultimate Frisbee teams warming up, and by controlling for whether teams seemed more or less athletic, researchers found that judgments of team cohesion significantly predicted win percentages.[53]

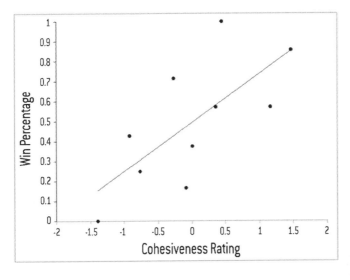

Figure 7. Group Cohesion and Winning

The second counter to social loafing is that cohesion increases if the task itself is both challenging and meaningful to the team members. Under such circumstances, members will exert as much effort together as they would individually. This phenomenon explains why responses to life-threatening situations, like the Farmy Army in Christchurch, can lift collective efforts to superhuman levels. Urgent and important tasks are powerfully motivating and trigger the ultra-social response in human groups.

The third counter to social loafing concerns how well the people on the team know each other. People are less inclined to loaf when working with people they know and with whom they are friends. Moreover, individual effort increases if the members are part of a highly successful or desirable team. Thus, when individuals win a place on a team whose members are highly respected and have a history of winning, the probability increases that they will exert their best efforts—as will their teammates.

Finally, the fourth antidote to social loafing concerns team size. As we saw above, smaller teams work more effectively than larger teams, because seeing the results of one's own efforts is easier on a small team than on a large one, and because social loafing is much harder to disguise when fewer people are involved.

I think of social cohesion as a form of capital that members invest to increase their own commitment to the team and to reduce social loafing (their own and others'). Cohesion depends on the hard, functional aspects of teamwork—as we saw in the Levi's case earlier—and cannot be simply mandated. Fairness, task design, and process design create the conditions in which social cohesion can flourish.

When combined, task and social cohesion wield a powerful influence on high-performance teamwork. A considerable body of literature has shown that cohesion improves group performance in the military, in health settings, in social groups, at work, and in the sporting arena. With regard to sports, a recent meta-analytic study (one that synthesizes the results of many separate studies—in this case over 100) found that cohesion positively affected team performance and league outcomes.[54] Teams whose members share a sense of mission and have feelings of camaraderie and regard for each other perform better than teams that don't. This maxim holds true across a wide variety of sports and cultures, even when controlling for age and gender.

But here is a major caveat: social cohesion, while important, doesn't lead to better performance by itself. One investigation sought to understand the causal relation between cohesion and performance. The reported patterns showed that performance exerted a stronger influence on cohesiveness than cohesiveness exerted on performance.[55] Cohesion develops as a consequence of clear goals, effective group norms, good leadership, and, very likely, the type of people you have on the team.

Low levels of cohesiveness limit the ability of a team to work effectively. Social relations that are distant, difficult, or nonexistent will slow communication and frustrate decision-making. In contrast, high levels of cohesion signify that team goals, norms, and decisions are likely to foster individuals' commitment and their motivation to strive for success. An environment in which people are supportive and interested in lifting the team's performance creates a positive spiral of increasing effort and satisfaction, which, in turn, increases the probability that the team's performance will continue to improve.

We'll look next at the rock star concept of human relations.

TRUST

The third soft element, trust, is a shifting, fluid construct, often invoked as the holy grail of social capital in human relationships. Yet its absence most clearly reveals its role, as the following story demonstrates.

The German owners of the Mercedes brand, Daimler, merged with the faltering American auto giant Chrysler in 1999. When the DaimlerChrysler union was announced, it was described as a merger of equals. Within a few months, however, staff morale began to drop precipitously, especially at Chrysler. Fights for status and position occurred between the Germans and Americans. The Europeans saw themselves as bringing rationality and process to the chaos of American manufacturing; the Americans saw arrogant, tin-eared executives trying to take over. *The Economist* reported a slew of departures, including those by talented Chrysler designers who defected in droves.[56] Market share began to slump, and despite optimistic talk from management, the stock price continued its downward trajectory (see chart below).

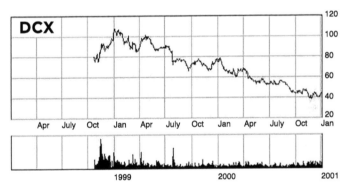

Period: Jan-5-1998 - Jan-4-2001

Figure 8. Falling Out of Love (Economist.com)

Within 18 months, DaimlerChrysler had a third-quarter loss of more than half a billion dollars, and its shared value had slipped 60%. The merger was ultimately deemed a failure, and in 2007, Chrysler was sold to a private equity firm.

But why did it all go so wrong?

Across the organization, and especially at the top, significant issues of trust sty-mied cooperation. Employees from both companies felt reluctant to work with each other, and the Chrysler staff felt especially fearful. Following the merger, a large number of Chrysler's executives either resigned or were replaced by their German counterparts. The Chrysler design staff that had defected to other firms had cited too many restrictions on their work as a reason for leaving. The two com-panies had different company cultures—one liked following rules, whereas the other was more informal. In addition, they practiced different decision-making and operating styles; the German business style clashed with the American business style, and the conflict fomented war between Daimler and Chrysler. Each side mis-trusted the other's intentions and came to believe that leadership had neither a clear plan nor any solution to the problems that Chrysler faced. In the end, a com-plete lack of trust undermined all efforts to make the partnership work.

Anyone who has worked with untrustworthy teammates or leaders will instantly ap-preciate how critical trust is. How can you dedicate yourself if you doubt the inten-tions of someone else? Fundamentally, trust requires vulnerability, making oneself open to other people's behavior in the positive belief that they will do what is expect-ed and won't undermine you—in other words, that they will exhibit *trustworthiness*. The best simple description of trustworthiness is that someone displays:[57]

Competence. He is capable of performing his job and can be trusted not to fail.

Benevolence. She will act in your best interests and honor your needs.

Integrity. He behaves in accordance with known principles and can be trusted to follow through on commitments.

One of the best-selling books on teamwork, *The 5 Dysfunctions of a Team* by Pat-rick Lencioni, noted that, "without [trust], teamwork is impossible."

Does trust really influence team dynamics? Studies on the relations between team trust and team performance have yielded conflicting and puzzling results. In some studies, groups with higher levels of trust performed no better than groups with lower levels of trust. These results indicate that trust, by itself, might not make a difference in the outcome.

On the other hand, an ingenious investigation of 92 teams of Dutch tax consultants determined exactly how trust operates to underpin better performance.[58] The researchers found that trust permitted the team to monitor its own performance honestly, which, in turn, boosted the overall effort. The implication is that a trusting team avoids the Ringelmann effect by making its own performance transparent and trusting its members to respond appropriately. This positivity underpins some of the findings about feedback and monitoring discussed previously and highlights the uniquely human need for transparency and shared commitment.

> Sales teams with the highest level of psychological safety performed better.

The mediating role of trust turns up in sports performance as well. A study of teams in a variety of sports (such as basketball and indoor soccer) revealed that trust among players and team coaches and leadership strongly influenced team cohesion, which, in turn, affected trust among the players themselves.[59] Taken together, trust explained more than 10% of the difference among teams' final rankings in various leagues.

Even in the data-oriented, geeky world of computer engineering, trust has been shown to matter more than individual skill to team performance. Google spent two years analyzing the behavior of 180 teams in a variety of functions, collecting real-time performance and questionnaire data. The researchers were especially interested in what differentiated the higher performing teams from the rest. The data demonstrated that psychological safety was the most critical.[60] Google sales teams with the highest level of psychological safety outperformed their revenue targets, on average, by 17%. Those with the lowest level of psychological safety underperformed their targets, on average, by 19%.

Psychological safety, which Google defined with the phrase, "Can we take risks on this team without feeling insecure or embarrassed?", is clearly akin to trust. Team members on unsafe teams will be reluctant to expose their own ideas or to challenge someone else's, and, although this reaction is understandable, it is harmful to good teamwork. The greater the trust that team members feel with one another (or the safer they feel), the more likely they are to admit mistakes, be honest about performance, push back on unworkable plans, and take on new roles.

Google's research found that psychological safety underlaid nearly every important dimension they investigated. Individuals on teams with high psychological safety were less likely to resign, brought in more revenue, and were rated effective by executives twice as often as their low-safety counterparts.

Finally, Google lists five factors that are essential to high-functioning teams, the first of which is psychological safety:

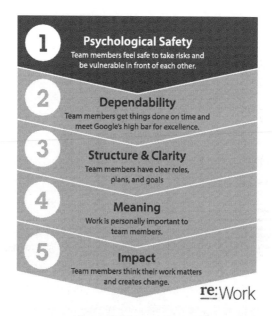

Figure 9. Google Rediscovers Teams

Trust assuredly doesn't work the way it is portrayed in Hollywood buddy movies, where heroes, thrust together by circumstance, initially dislike each other. After a near-death experience, they realize they can trust each other, symbolized by a gaze into the middle distance and a manly speech admitting grudging respect and minimal thanks. Trust is an odd human characteristic, in that it must be given before it is received, thus requiring individuals to display vulnerability. Trust also requires people to act with integrity and benevolence. The conditions in which trust flourishes emerge not from games like trust falls, but from honest, open appraisals of performance, a dogged determination to improve, and a commitment to the success of one's colleagues.

Nor is trust a binary on/off event. Rather, it evolves from the accumulated experience of tens and hundreds of interactions. Trust may sound soft, but it is one of the toughest of all team capabilities.

COMMUNICATION

In 1978, in Portland, Oregon, United Airlines Flight 173 with 189 people on board circled the landing airport while the pilot explored a minor landing-gear problem. In itself, the problem wasn't serious enough to prevent the plane from landing, but the captain spent 45 minutes fiddling with manuals and levers and burned through all the plane's fuel. Realizing too late what he had done, he crash-landed miles short of the runway in a wooded area, killing 10 people. Investigators determined that the two other crew personnel in the cockpit knew of the issue, repeatedly mentioned to the pilot that fuel was low, but failed to assert themselves or take control for fear of causing conflict.[61]

The Portland incident isn't an isolated one. Staying with the aviation theme, a similar, possibly apocryphal, story describes a plane's crashing into an airport structure as it was taxiing along the runway. The cockpit voice recorder revealed that, in talking among themselves, the other crew members noted the plane was off course. They talked to each other about how the captain was heading to the wrong runway, then off the runway, and then into the building. The crew clearly identified that something was wrong and were heard checking and confirming the correct runway and route, but they did nothing as the captain ignored their sotto voce comments. They paid for their reticence with their lives. Analysis revealed that the captain had dropped dead from a heart attack at the start of the taxiway, with his hands on the controls and his eyes wide open.

Even though such situations may seem outlandish, human psychology potentiates the subservient responses that the two crews showed their leaders. As group-living animals, humans operate in various hierarchies; sustaining one's place in a hierarchy requires deferring to authority and leadership, especially in times of stress.

Quasi-military organizations like airlines (note the uniforms, caps, and braid) emphasize the chain of command and compliance with legitimate orders. Nevertheless, these types of incidents prompted airlines (and some air forces) to design training programs to counter this psychology. They created crew resource management (CRM) programs, formal and compulsory training for cockpit crews. Through seminars, simulations, and practical exercises, the CRM process teaches self-awareness, enhanced situational awareness, assertiveness, decision-making, conflict management, and listening. This training has proven its effectiveness in changing behavior between individuals and within groups.[62] Fire service crews, hospital operating rooms, and the military have also implemented variants of these communications training modules.

CRM is eminently successful in changing behavior because it emphasizes practical skills and teaches verbal routines that individuals and teams can learn easily. Respectful and helpful communication is the goal, as demonstrated in the following example from the International Association of Fire Chiefs' CRM manual:[63]

1. Opening or attention getter—Address the individual. "Hey Bob," or "Captain Smith," or "Boss, I've noticed ..." or whatever will get the person's attention.
2. State your concern—Express your analysis of the situation in a direct manner while owning your emotions about it: "I'm concerned that we haven't enough fuel to fly around this storm system," or "I'm worried that the roof might collapse."
3. State the problem as you see it—"We're showing only 40 minutes of fuel left," or "This building is all wood construction and we may have fire extension into the roof structure."
4. State one or more solutions—"There are three airports we can divert to and refuel," or "I think we should pull some iron off and use the thermal imaging camera before we commit crews."
5. Obtain agreement (or buy-in)—"Agree with that idea, Captain?"

One of the most innovative investigations of team communications was undertaken by the MIT Human Dynamics Lab, which used wearable electronic sensors to collect data on team member communication behaviors—tone of voice, movements, body position, to whom and how long they talked.[64] They didn't measure the content of the communications, however. Using powerful statistical techniques to search through the reams of data collected, they discovered that the most productive teams had a revealing communications-data signature which characterized a team's energy, engagement, and exploration. Measuring these three dimensions enabled the MIT investigators to distinguish among teams in terms of goal attainment, member satisfaction, and even profit-making.

Energy was measured by the number and the nature of exchanges among team members, exchanges that could be as short as a comment or acknowledgment—for example, a "yes" or a nod of the head, or as long as a full-fledged, team meeting. The better teams engaged in more exchanges than did poorly performing teams.

Furthermore, the researchers found that not all communications are created equal. The best communication happens face-to-face. Phone calls and videoconferences are second best, but they come with a caveat: they are less effective as more people participate (see the earlier discussion concerning the increasing size of a team producing diminishing returns). Emailing and texting are the least effective forms of exchange, a lesson that 99% of modern organizations should take to heart.

Overstating the importance of this finding would be difficult. Because humans have evolved to deal with one another in person, the rule is that more communication is better than less. Moreover, people favor the full range of grunts, smirks, nods, eye-glances, and shrugs that come with face-to-face communication. In fact, in-person communication may matter more in the modern electronic economy than it used to. Technology can produce stilted, transactional, and poorly rehearsed teamwork because team members have little to no social cohesion, even if they are dedicated to the task. Therefore, far-flung teams benefit from tools and from events like off-sites and conferences to build cohesion, team energy, and communication.

Engagement, MIT's second dimension of communication, was a measure of the distribution of energy (the number of interactions) among team members. If the team members displayed high energy, engagement was strong, and performance tended to be strong as well. In contrast, partially engaged teams were lopsided with knots of high-energy communicators and isolated individuals, a configuration that predicted poorer performance. When the researchers examined teams' investment decisions, they observed that partially engaged teams made less profitable decisions than did their fully engaged counterparts.

Both energy and engagement carry implications for virtual or distributed teams, in which sustaining face-to-face connection is difficult, and the members barely know each other. These teams start with a surfeit of task cohesion (the task is all that connects the members) but a woeful lack of social cohesion. The MIT work clearly showed that investing in relationships and increasing the frequency of communication pays off.

That technology has not contributed more in this area is surprising. Although so-called team technologies like Slack, Sqwiggle, or HipChat exist, they do not emphasize team development, tending instead to focus on coordination and project management. Although instituting private team or project chat boards, shared documents, and coordinated schedules and timetables is useful, these technologies have failed to address the social cohesion element.

However, innovative tools are now beginning to emerge. For instance, a new team-building startup called Know Your Crew (KYC) recently launched a platform aimed at increasing cohesion, energy, and engagement. The KYC tool has team members complete quizzes that turn into games that let them accumulate points for responding to questions like, "Who has climbed Mount Kilimanjaro?" Underneath its game-like front end, the platform has sophisticated analytics that track a range of metrics, such as team energy, optimism, and self-efficacy. Especially useful in large corporate environments and for dispersed and virtual teams, the popularity of these types of social technologies is likely to grow.

One of the best places to see energy and engagement in action is in the kitchens of well-run restaurants. Working under the pressure of high demand and a nightly, ruthless dissection of their performance by diners, great kitchens are a tightly choreographed, interdependent production line. They have to be able to respond quickly to disasters, cover for each other's errors, and meet tight deadlines, all in pursuit of superb food. The best kitchens employ a call-and-response cadence as the chef calls out orders coming in from the floor. Cooks call back acknowledgment of the orders. Crew members share the state of their stations and let each other know (often bluntly) to "hurry up with that turbot." Further, the crew maintains *situational awareness*, the group sense of what is happening and what might happen, through this swirl of conversation, observation, and updating. Kitchen crews can stay together for decades, build tight performance routines, and develop a deep appreciation of each other's strengths and foibles, all in service to the chef's vision and their combined reputation.

MIT's third critical communications component was exploration. Higher-performing teams have more, and more frequent, outside connections. As one might expect, exploration is a differentiator for creative teams, such as teams that are responsible for innovation and thus seek fresh perspectives.

In keeping with our evolutionary narrative about teams, none of the MIT dimensions function continuously. Teams oscillate—that is, activity ebbs and flows in tune with the demands of the workflow and of outside pressure—so creative teams might be strong on exploration at the start of a project and increase energy and engagement as the project focuses and heads towards delivery.

The takeaway is that communication functions as a lifeblood for the work of the team and is an indicator for the internal health of the team. Of course, not all communication need be out loud, but the evidence shows that more communication between team members and their environment beats less.

CONFLICT

As noted earlier, cohesion relates to both the relationships within the team, social cohesion, and the shared focus on the mission, task cohesion. In working with senior leadership teams, I found that social cohesion functioned a bit like sugar: too little and the team was conflicted and grumpy, and the members didn't coalesce. On the other hand, too much cohesion was sickly sweet. It depressed team performance because the executives tended to avoid conflict and agree with each other.[65]

The traditional term for this phenomenon is *groupthink*, a term coined by Irving Janis to describe the tendency of cohesive groups to settle too quickly for a unanimous viewpoint, thereby extinguishing their willingness to question the shared point of view.[66] One of Janis' most quoted examples was the group of advisers who worked with President John F. Kennedy when he decided to invade Cuba in the ill-fated adventure now known as the Bay of Pigs. Self-assured, supremely confident, and unusually cohesive, the group fed on its own ego and that of the charismatic young president, completely misreading the situation and the chance of failure. They ignored contrary evidence and pressed ahead with a doomed invasion plan.

Although groupthink has been a useful model, subsequent research suggests that the reality is a little more nuanced. Daniel Bayne describes the process as follows:

> A group of decision-makers enjoys some early successes and develops an exaggerated sense of their own competence. Eventually, they encounter a situation that's beyond their actual abilities and end up in over their heads. When they finally realize their predicament, they perceive any corrective action as a choice between losses (relative to the unreasonably positive outcome they originally anticipated). When faced with a choice between losses, people tend to favor riskier courses of action. Thus, the group not only fails to correct their error, they actively make decisions that make the situation worse.[67]

When I was conducting research into senior leadership teams, and in my coaching work since then, I found the reluctance of teams to reflect on their own performance astounding. Teams moved from decision to decision with almost no focus on critical evaluation or on after-action review. The more senior the team, the less likely they were to examine their performance critically. Partly, this reluctance was the result of the confidence that accrues to those at the top of organizations—a confidence that British psychologist Tomas Chamorro-Premuzic points out should not be confused with competence.[68] But the reluctance is also due to another factor that contributes to poor performance: sustaining healthy conflict.

Generally speaking, team conflict shows up when the team is clarifying its task and initial plans. The task is the one thing that unites everyone until the team develops an identity and shared norms. Thus, task conflicts first arise from differences in opinions about the mission or its execution; furthermore, the level of conflict can rise when members debate incompatible solutions and ideas.

The potential for conflict is most obvious when a team gathers for the first time. With little knowledge of what other people will contribute and an urge to establish themselves in the social hierarchy, team members typically leap towards solutions, indiscriminately offering ideas and competing for air time, a phenomenon known as *flight to task*. For most teams, this period is uncomfortable and unpleasant, and many people will seek to minimize it, defer to the natural loudmouths, or withdraw and wait until others reach a consensus. As difficult as flight to task might be to resolve, leaving it unresolved keeps a team stuck, circling around solutions and unable to reach a decision or move forward as team members continue to argue and debate.

On the other hand, engaging in a debate over ideas sounds healthy and is decidedly the opposite of groupthink. Does task conflict enhance performance, or does it lead to failure? Studies reveal that task conflict benefits the team by forging greater clarity with regard to task and goals, providing diverging perspectives on solutions, uncovering new information and insights, curtailing premature decisions, and sparking innovation. In support of this view, one of the foremost scientists investigating team conflict, Karen Jehn, has shown that task conflict is indeed positive for team performance, but only when relationships among team members are strong and the team knows how to manage conflict.[69]

> Communication functions as a lifeblood for the work of the team and is an indicator for the internal health of the team.

In fact, reliable patterns of task, relationships, and conflict predict team performance.[70] When task conflict is high, but relationships are strong and the team is skilled at managing arguments, team performance is enhanced. In contrast, conflict-management skill is degraded by emotion when the relationships among members fray or are shaky from the outset.

In summary, the objective is not to stifle argument or dissent. Teams that are overly agreeable and suppress discord at almost any cost perform much worse than do teams who argue productively. Learning to cope with conflict is a relatively straightforward skill that we teach when coaching high-performing management teams. Although we use a number of tools, the basic six-step framework is simple:

1. CLARIFY THE QUESTION AND FOCUS ON FACTS AND EVIDENCE.

In certain executive team meetings that I've attended, I've been struck by how ill-disciplined team member behaviors are—interjecting remarks, talking over each other, playing with phones or laptops, engaging in side conversations—a childish and egocentric set of behaviors. But these are minor-league annoyances compared to the most egregious sin: not having a clue what the argument is about.

Some of my most effective coaching interventions have forced teams to clarify questions, decisions, or problems. After the issues have been defined to everyone's understanding, the arguments can progress.

At that point, the rule becomes: the more facts, the better. In the absence of objective, current data, team members will push opinions at one another, opinions that tend to reflect their personal values. Arguments about opinions frequently end in a stalemate since no objective data are available to resolve the problem. Moreover, members without a stake in the argument are likely to harden their views towards the dissenting team member(s), thereby eroding trust.

2. GENERATE MULTIPLE ALTERNATIVES.

Examining as much evidence and data as can be mustered, successful teams work to formulate a number of theories or scenarios that explain the information. Various explanations or multiple options allow team members to shift positions without losing face, thus fostering more creative solutions. Several ideas are better than one, and discussing legitimate choices produces better decisions.[71]

3. KEEP GROUNDING THE DISCUSSION IN SHARED GOALS.

An earlier discussion emphasized the importance of shared goals in managing the hard factors of team success. Team members need to remain aware of their common goal and to direct any conflict towards achieving that goal. Goals that transcend any one person's reach can inspire awe and stop arguments from becoming turf battles.

One of our exercises asks team members to work through a ladder of what ifs: "What if we fix this problem? Where does that take us?" and "What if we can fix that problem as well? Where does that take us?" Usually, the exercise leads to considering the larger, higher-level goals to which team members have already committed—and collaborating to reach a shared goal tends to remove defensiveness.

4. USE HUMOR.

Using humor is an effective strategy for creating a collaborative and optimistic at-mosphere. In addition, many teams use humor as a way to relieve tension and to deliver negative feedback in a tactful, face-saving way.

5. BALANCE THE POWER STRUCTURE.

A number of the more dramatic corporate failures over the last decade have re-sulted from the influence of dominant (and sometimes unethical) bosses: Enron, WorldCom, Yahoo, and Hewlett-Packard come to mind. In each case, the CEO domi-nated the leadership and hence, the organization.

One of the more remarkable investigations of CEOs' impacts on organizational suc-cess found that most people accepted decisions they disagreed with if they felt that the process was fair. For senior executives, fairness was seen as an opportu-nity to have their input considered seriously. Another aspect of fairness revealed by the study was the belief that the ultimate decision had been driven by facts and sound analysis, not by personality and politics.

6. SEEK CONSENSUS WITH QUALIFICATION.

In the investigation discussed above, all of the teams that were effective at han-dling conflict put significant effort into reaching, but not forcing, consensus. If the full group was unable to reach an agreement, the CEO or the most relevant execu-tive would consider the group's input and then make the final decision. This ap-proach met the criterion of perceived fairness, as described above, without need-lessly delaying decisions.[72]

HOW TO JOIN THE HARD AND THE SOFT

*Do not be too hard, lest you be broken. Do not
be too soft, lest you be squeezed.*

— RAli ibn Abi Talib

What could be more useful for building teams than a simple recipe for combining the essential components of a successful team? Researchers, consultants, and organizations have applied many approaches, all of which share a few critical elements.

One of the most well-known team researchers was Harvard Professor Richard Hackman.[73] As a young man, Hackman played basketball and wound up coaching the Harvard women's basketball team for many years. These experiences provided him with firsthand knowledge about team building, from which he identified four key elements:

1. **Real Team:** Real teams have clear boundaries and are interdependent; they also have enough stability of membership to give members time to learn how to work together.

2. **Compelling Direction:** The team's overall purpose is challenging (which energizes members), clear, and consequential.

3. **Enabling Structure:** Hackman thought three structural features were key to competent teamwork. First, the team task should involve completing a full mission, as opposed to accomplishing only bits and pieces of the whole. And, in a related vein, members should be free to make decisions about work procedures. Second, the team should be as small as possible and exhibit technical and interpersonal skill. Finally, the team should clearly and

explicitly define what constitutes desirable and unacceptable behavior.

4. **Supportive Context:** Hackman also believed that even a well-constructed team would fail if the organization failed to provide an ongoing development program, a suitable reward system, and a feedback system that allowed team access to appropriate data.

If the above doesn't sound enough like rocket science, then help is at hand. Gordon Curphy has developed a simple model of the requisite elements for team success called The Rocket Model.[74]

Perhaps because Curphy had served with the United States Air Force, he adopted a space-flight metaphor for organizing the key aspects of team performance. The Rocket Model likens building a team to building a rocket, in that both ventures consist of several stages. I find this framework especially useful because it integrates the hard elements of team performance (structure, skills, and goals) with the softer elements (cohesion, communication, etc.). Importantly, the model is both descriptive and prescriptive: it can prescribe how to develop a new team from scratch, and it can diagnose problems or identify opportunities in an existing team.

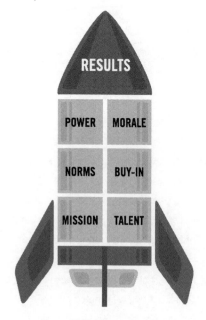

Figure 10. The Rocket Model

1. CONTEXT

First, Curphy emphasizes the importance of context. All teams function in an operating space or context—the set of conditions, constraints, and expectations that shape the team's mission, as well as how its members should adapt and behave. The operating context of a film crew in a war zone differs considerably from that of a film crew operating in a studio, and the differences must be taken into account when designing and creating the team. Because team members may carry different beliefs or assumptions about which elements of the context are most important and about how the team should tackle them, it behooves team leaders to guide the members in developing a common appreciation of the world in which they operate. In the military, this is termed "situational awareness." In the world of work, it may require building a shared awareness of vendors, markets, regulators, customers, and so on. Instilling a strong, shared sense of context facilitates defining the team's mission.

2. MISSION AND TALENT

The stage that matters most in firing a rocket is the first one, which, for teams, Curphy calls Mission and Talent. This stage consumes nearly all the fuel and is the largest component of the structure. If the rocket cannot build up the tremendous speed required to defeat gravity's pull, the rest of the rocket, and the mission, are irrelevant.

So too with teams. Without a purpose and the talent to achieve it, a team cannot get going at all. While that seems elementary, startups stumble all the time because the core team lacks appropriate talent, or the best group of people possible flounder and fail to define what they have to deliver.

And in keeping with the advice I proffered above, that form follows function, it is the mission that should determine the skills and talents the team requires. Mission and context together will shape the rules and informal norms by which the team operates, and the tools and resources necessary to complete its tasks. In fact, setting common goals and aligning them to individual and organizational priorities, to performance standards, and to the team's overall purpose is perhaps the most important work a team can perform.

Having defined the mission, teams must identify the appropriate roles needed to deliver it. When building a football team, this work is already done, and each position on the field has expectations of the skills and talents required to excel. In building a startup team, these decisions can become much more difficult, and involve tradeoffs and overlap. Nonetheless, the concept of talent connotes more than just competence or skill—an optimal number of well-defined roles, along with people who are prepared to devote their energy to the mission and to supporting one another, are essential. It also should involve a consideration of the personalities of the team members and the manner in which they will work together, a point we'll explore in depth below.

Ernest Shackleton, British Antarctic explorer of the last century, spent weeks choosing the men who would accompany him on his voyage to the bottom of the earth. He interviewed each man, drew up lists of their characteristics and experience, and pondered long about how they might fit together on a journey that would last years. A good job he did: the ship was trapped in ice and destroyed, and Shackleton led the crew on the most arduous survival experience ever documented. Would that modern organizations put as much thought into choosing people as Shackleton did.

3. NORMS

All teams function under the constraint of rules, whether they are written down or not, or even whether the team acknowledges them. For example, when I started on the night crew of a factory producing milk powder, everyone shook the hand of every other team member before every single shift. On the first night, I thought this was because I was new; on the second, I thought they were making game of me; by the second week, I came to accept it as just the thing we did before the shift to establish connection.

Informal norms, like the handshake ritual, constitute tacit rules about "how we do things around here." Norms exert a strong influence on team behavior, but because they are implicit and evolve over time, they are often unremarked. After the team's mission has been specified and appropriate team members have been selected, norms define the team operating culture. Importantly, norms will develop in any event: smart teams will take the time to think through the pros and cons of how things get done around here, making sure they help the team deliver on the mission.

Formal procedures or rules explicitly identify and codify how the team will conduct itself so that all team members attend to the same conventions. For the most part, these rules delineate operations to standardize daily activity. Among the operations that team norms might define are the following:

a) Who does what, and how does work get passed to others?
b) What decisions must be made, and how will the team make them?
c) How does the work get done?
d) When, where, and how often will the team meet?

It is always worth clarifying and reviewing the formal and informal rules that govern team behavior. Recall the finding that good teams have enough trust to display performance and process transparently; the very best teams regularly reflect on what they do and how they are doing it.

4. BUY-IN

Just because team members have a shared mission, it does not necessarily imply that all members are committed to it. Buy-in is a shared psychological state: the degree to which team members are both *committed to* and *engaged in* team goals, roles, and norms. Teams with buy-in are genuinely enthused by their tasks, and those around them notice the team's positive tone and energetic participation. Typically, buy-in emerges through a process of give-and-take negotiating among leaders and team members. Once again, testing team buy-in consciously and transparently will bring dividends later.

5. POWER

Curphy defines power as the control of resources that are in high demand and necessary to achieve the task. Equipment, time, funds, and even the authority to make decisions all constitute power. No team can function if it doesn't have the tools needed to do the job, and dysfunctional teams can become preoccupied with what they don't have. In contrast, successful teams are not only clear about the resources they need, but they will exert the influence necessary to acquire them.

6. MORALE

Moreover, for a team to achieve maximum effectiveness, it must transcend individual differences and power struggles and address conflict in a healthy manner. When morale falls below a tipping point, teams become dysfunctional. Therefore, effective teams invest time and effort in behaving benevolently towards and establishing trust with other team members, thereby facilitating high morale. High morale underpins team performance, satisfaction, and enjoyment. Being proud to be part of the team and celebrating wins are indicators that the team can resolve their conflicts and value working together.

My consulting firm uses The Rocket Model both as a checklist to help in the design of teams and as a diagnostic for teams already operating. Because it so carefully walks teams and leaders through the essential elements of effective team operations, The Rocket Model provides an excellent tool to use in team coaching assignments, or for team leaders interested in lifting team performance.

VIRTUAL TEAMS

With the rise of technology, the rise of borderless commerce, and the rise of team working, it is inevitable that teams will span time zones, nationalities, and technologies. Virtuality, when team members do not work in the same physical space, is rapidly becoming normal for many workers.

Virtual teams (VTs) offer a great insight into why the hard and soft need to be well managed in all teams, but, in fact, soft factors may actually require even closer attention in virtual teams.

For example, consider some of the modern team working platforms, like Slack. On one hand, Slack promotes transparency, in that all team members can see the chats on the channel, and it encourages frequent communication, which increases satisfaction and decreases social loafing.[75] But technology also creates lags in information exchange and slows down decision-making.[76]

To make virtual teams work at their best, the same rules discussed above still apply. Goal clarity turns out to be vital, along with making sure that everyone on the channel understands both their own and other's roles. VTs that establish goals early in their life cycle show increased cohesion and better performance.[77] Sticking to predictable and regular cycles—establishing a reliable rhythm for the team's operations—also produces better team performance.

Soft factors are also vital. Teams whose leaders spend more time building relationships with distant workers do better, and if the leader is also good at connecting people within the team, these connections will enhance cohesion and performance. There is also a benefit for the leader: leaders who focused on relationships rather than task-based factors were perceived as more intelligent, creative, and original.[78] In contrast, functional leaders were described as authoritative, task focused, and arrogant.

> Soft factors are more critical for virtual team success.

The evidence is quite clear that time invested in developing connections between people in the team results in greater trust and stronger commitment and cohesion and reduces the transaction costs that inevitably accompany virtual teams. Information exchange between members is strongly related to perceptions of competence. In the virtual world, sharing is very close to caring.[79]

8

THE DEEP DYNAMICS OF TEAMS

Yo Yo Yo Son,
You ever felt a funny vibe,
What you supposed to do?
➤ *"In Too Deep" by Nas (featuring Nature)*

Earlier discussions have addressed the hard aspects of team effectiveness; patterns of workflow and the shape and nature of the task are critical determinants of team design and performance. Further discussions have considered the soft elements of teamwork: the effects of cohesion, communication, and a team's ability to deal with conflict. The next step addresses the deep components of teamwork: elements such as values and personality. This topic is less straightforward than the preceding ones, but based on my own years of practice and research, I am convinced that engaging with the deep components is crucial to helping teams reach breakthrough performance.

To explore the deep aspects of teamwork, consider the challenge that Elon Musk has posed: he wants to have a manned flight land on Mars by 2025 and to establish a colony there during his lifetime. The oddities of celestial alignment are such that waiting for the planets to align, considering the space journey there and back, and allowing for time on the surface of Mars mean that the entire mission will last nearly three years.

This project would mean that for days, weeks, months, and years, four people would be cooped up together in a small space, perhaps the size of a modest two-bedroom apartment—and time would pass slowly. How on earth (literally, on Earth) would one select a crew to undertake such a mission?

If the decision were left to the team members themselves, the resulting team might not be optimal. People notice each other initially by surface-level characteristics such as skin color, gender, age, and so on. Team members are inclined to be attracted to one another more when they are similar. That is, during the beginning stages of working together, people find it easier to connect with individuals who seem similar to them, in terms of characteristics like language, ethnicity, education, or experience.

However, as team members spend more time together, they go beyond the surface level as they talk, work, and watch each other's behavior. These opportunities, along with the passing of time, permit the strength of initial stereotypes and assumptions to diminish; instead, deep-level characteristics like personality and values emerge as es-

> The more diverse the team's values, the less cohesive and effective the team.

sential for developing social cohesion and enhancing performance.[80] In a study of university students, teams with members who shared significant *personal values*, like tradition, power, or altruism, reported more cohesion when compared to their less similar counterparts.[81] Greater value diversity was associated with reduced cohesion and team efficacy. In contrast, evidence from student teams and manufacturing teams found that having members who differ on *personality variables* (like sociability or detail focus) produced stronger cohesion and better performance.[82] It's worth diving into the deep dynamics of teams to explore how personality and values impact team success, and how to use these variables to build effective teams.

PERSONALITY

Psychologists love to classify people, usually using psychological tests. Neurotics, for example, sit on a continuum ranging from anxious, despondent, fretful, high-strung, insecure, irritable, moody, self-pitying, self-punishing, and unstable, to calm, contented, patient, relaxed, stable, uncritical, secure, and self-satisfied.

But does a personality test score actually reveal anything about what people want, say, do, and feel, or how they lead their lives in the real world? In short, yes, it does.

Studies have shown that people whose test scores present them as neurotic tend to die earlier and experience fewer positive feelings than do those whose scores imply emotional stability. And neuroticism scores also predict depression, divorce, and heart disease.[83, 84] Other personality attributes, like sociability or conscientiousness, are just as predictive of life events. Personality is as consequential to life outcomes as IQ and socioeconomic status.

Personality psychology had twin births. The first occurred in 19th century European psychiatry. The early writers—Freud especially—believed that the most important generalizations to assert about people were that everyone is somewhat neurotic and that the most crucial of life's challenges was to overcome one's neuroses. Freud was a genius in many ways, but his belief in universal neuroses has been challenged.

Meanwhile, in England, Sir Francis Galton, cousin to Charles Darwin and a brilliant polymath, found the ideas of his cousin compelling and began exploring how people can be so similar yet display marked individual differences. He then set about measuring some of these differences, which he regarded as personality traits. (Less happily, he formulated odd ideas about racial differences and came to believe in eugenics.) Galton's measurement strategy was methodical and systematic. His brilliant insight was that every human language encodes socially meaningful personality differences by providing trait descriptions of people. Thus, one person might be described as gregarious, while his/her little brother is characterized as insular. A third individual might be known as a serious and quiet person who is also calm and self-assured.

What Galton called his lexical framework attracted little attention until Gordon Allport and Henry Odbert expanded on the idea.[85] Allport and Odbert sifted through two comprehensive English dictionaries and extracted 17,953 personality-describing words, which they reduced to 4,500 adjectives that they considered to describe observable and relatively stable traits. This extraordinary piece of work laid the foundation for understanding how human beings use a simple, basic framework to describe other people.

Ten years later, Raymond Cattell reduced the Allport-Odbert list to 171 terms, and asked people to rate their friends, colleagues, and relatives using the shorter list.

Analyzing these ratings using the emerging technology of computers and the statistical tool of factor analysis, Cattell identified 35 clusters of personality traits.[86]

The next breakthrough in this work came in the 1960s. Two US Air Force researchers applied Cattell's trait measure to analyzing data from eight large military samples. What they found were five broad, underlying factors. Their work was replicated by a researcher named Norman,[87] who not only replicated the five major factors, but gave them new names: Surgency (an old-fashioned term that means positivity and sociability), Agreeableness, Conscientiousness, Emotional Stability, and Culture.

Science prefers simple explanations—less is often more. Results of the ongoing research that has succeeded Norman's efforts have disclosed that most of the broad-level variations in human behavior or its underlying characteristics can be efficiently described using only Norman's five big factors. And because psychologists are not famous for their dazzling branding skills, this framework became known as the Big Five Model of personality. It holds up across nations, cultures, ethnicities, and gender, and it has become the basic working model for how humans differ in their approaches to life.

The easiest way to remember the Big Five is by using the acronym OCEAN:

O Openness: Narrow and unimaginative versus curious and creative. High scorers are artistic and curious, and they like variety and intellectual pursuits. Low scorers tend to be practical and concerned with the tried and true.

C Conscientiousness: Impulsive and careless versus dependable and rule-following. High scorers make plans and are thorough and careful. Low scorers tend to be impulsive and spontaneous; they may be sloppy and take risks.

E Extraversion: Active, sociable, and outgoing versus quiet, reserved, and unassertive. High scorers are gregarious, energetic, and talkative. Low scorers are quiet, tend to keep to themselves, and interact with smaller circles of friends.

A Agreeableness: Inflexible, unconcerned with others' feelings, cold, and blunt versus tactful, caring, warm, and empathic. High scorers tend to promote social bonds and care about other people's feelings. Low scorers are direct, aloof, and inclined to treat relationships as a means to an end.

N Neuroticism: Tense, self-critical, and emotional versus calm and assured. High scorers tend to be pessimistic and worried about how others see them; low scorers are relaxed and easy-going.

How do people get their personalities? The answer seems to be that personality is partly inherited and partly developed. That personality appears to persist across the lifespan has been established—people who are neurotic when they are young are likely to be more neurotic than their peers when they are old (although more comfortable with their anxieties). On the other hand, people's personalities can and do alter over time, though typically, not by much and usually in similar ways. For example, a significant life event, like marriage, can lead to personality change.[88] Marriage helps individuals mature (which means they learn more self-control) because they get feedback from marriage partners and because they invest in social roles that lead them to moderate their personalities.[89]

As we saw above, personality leads people to flock together and to concentrate in similar roles and careers. That might explain why, for instance, we observe personality concentrations in the landscape. For example, the United States was first settled by Europeans who landed on the Eastern seaboard and established businesses, towns, and infrastructure on that coast. As the population of European immigrants grew, more adventurous and exploratory types began to push westward, into the Great Plains and towards the California coast. Does this distinction imply that the people who remained on the East Coast were less open and more aware of the risks they would face by setting off into the great unknown (i.e., more neurotic)? Studies using the Big Five have produced maps that show the clustering of different personality types across the country:[90] as Figure 11 illustrates, New Yorkers indeed do display more neuroticism than do Californians, who are more relaxed and creative. As for countries, so for teams as well. Birds of a feather tend to flock together.

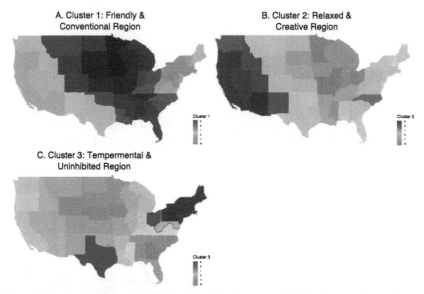

A. Cluster 1: Friendly & Conventional Region

B. Cluster 2: Relaxed & Creative Region

C. Cluster 3: Tempermental & Uninhibited Region

Figure 11. Personality Maps of the USA http://www.livescience.com/40511-most-neurotic-creative-states-revealed-in-us-personality-map.html

Personalities provide the road that people travel as they navigate the social world and come to know and understand one another. Personalities define individuals, at least in the eyes of others. As a result, a team member's characteristic patterns of thinking, feeling, and behaving will affect the team's performance through a variety of processes, ranging from the strength of each member's desire to get ahead to how each member approaches tasks, whether the approaches mesh within the team, and how effectively the team deals with problems. Further, how members form relationships and interact with one another on a daily basis will also influence the team.

Some inconsistency might be expected—teams are dynamic entities and, in the real world, people move in and out of them, projects are put on hold or accelerated, goals change, and managers can be either skilled or incompetent. Yet, a wealth of research has investigated the effects of team members' personalities on team performance; the results are sometimes contradictory but, overall, show a strong effect.

PERSONALITY AND TEAM PERFORMANCE

One of the side effects of identifying the Big Five was a flourishing of research into personality. Using the common model, researchers could begin to explore and compare how individual human characteristics affect love, health, work, and of most interest to us, teams.

Early results were equivocal. Some studies showed a strong link between personality and team performance, while others did not. However, a 1998 study conducted by two well-known researchers, Murray Barrick and Michael Mount yielded positive results for the impact of personality on team performance.[91] Specifically, Barrick and Mount found that teams composed of highly conscientious individuals performed better than teams with low conscientious members. They also showed that teams with higher agreeableness ratings, who were more emotionally stable, tended to exhibit higher performance. Finally, they found that teams built from members with high extraversion scores, and who had high emotional stability scores, sustained better performance for longer.

A decade later, in 2007, Suzanne Bell of DePaul University conducted the most comprehensive review to date of all findings relating personality to team performance.[92] By examining the results of dozens of previous investigations, Bell found that team-level personality predicts team performance. Importantly for our purposes, she saw that the effect of personality was weaker for laboratory-based studies conducted with students than it was for teams in the working world. I think this is a point worth reiterating: personality has a stronger effect on team performance in the real world than in the lab. Although the reasons are related to the fact that the team exercises in the lab were constructed by researchers who don't work with real teams, the result underscores how relevant personality is for working teams.

But what aspects of personality matter more?

Like Barrick and Mount's results, the largest and most consistent of Bell's findings were for conscientiousness. Teams with a larger number of highly conscientious members demonstrated greater performance. This finding is understandable because highly conscientious team members are typically hardworking, responsible, rule-following, organized, and task oriented.

Bell found similar results when she investigated the role of agreeableness. Increased levels of agreeableness tended to be associated with higher team performance, although the finding isn't as strong as for conscientiousness. Researchers in Taiwan, who studied cohesion in 133 teams working in the semiconductor industry, also found support for this phenomenon: high levels of agreeableness and openness to experience, combined with low levels of neuroticism, were associated with increases in both cohesion and helping behavior among teammates.[93] Additionally, Bell also found the "bad apple" effect: one disagreeable member can disrupt the social harmony of the entire team and cause team performance to suffer.

> The task the team has to deliver determines the type of people needed.

In short, better-performing teams comprise calm, disciplined, and warm people.

The next strongest relation Bell found was between openness and team performance, although the effect was smaller. This finding suggests that having team members who are creative, broadminded, and willing to try new things produces better team results. Team members who possess these characteristics will adapt to new situations, build upon each other's ideas, and look for alternative solutions to problems.

I think, however, that these findings reinforce the idea that the task the team has to deliver determines the type of people who are likely to do better. For example, after a volcanic eruption dumped millions of tons of corrosive ash into a hydropower waterway (yes, in NZ again), the expensive power generating turbines wore out 10 times sooner than normal. Since each one is bespoke and costs millions of dollars, the company was desperate to solve the problem. We quickly learned to stage the involvement of the highly conscientious, detail-oriented water engineers. They were extremely demotivating during the ideation phase. They kept slowing the process with interminable technical discussions and pooh-poohed most ideas as unworkable. Therefore, we introduced the engineers only at the start, in building out an understanding of the problems, and again at the end, when it came time to evaluate the ideas.

GOOD TEAM PLAYERS AND BAD APPLES

One of the best ways to observe the impact of personality on team performance comes from seeing what happens to a team when a negative personality appears.

As we saw earlier, Terrell Owens may have been athletically gifted, but as a team player, he was definitely a bad apple. Bad apples are team members who damage the team's esprit de corps or prevent the team from developing trust. They wield disproportionate influence on team functioning. For example, a dominant team member can monopolize conversations and prevent teammates from contributing to decisions or defining team goals. Ultimately, this behavior damages team performance. And it's true that a bad apple can spoil the barrel: research on mood contagion and unhappiness suggests that even one poorly adjusted member can influence the entire group.[94]

Will Felps and his colleagues described three types of behavior that characterize bad apples:[95]

1. Withholding effort by shirking work, being deliberately tardy, or otherwise not pulling one's weight.
2. Consistently expressing negative emotions, like anxiety or pessimism.
3. Violating established interpersonal norms by acting in a spiteful manner, denigrating the team or its identity, or engaging in thoughtless pranks.

As psychologist Roy Baumeister has observed, "bad is stronger than good."[96i] Human beings have an innate bias towards attaching more weight to negative feelings, events, and situations than to positive ones. For example, Felps relates that his wife experienced her workplace as cold and hostile until one of her coworkers, a particularly acerbic and derisive man, contracted an illness that kept him away from work for several days; during his absence, the environment changed:

> "And when he was gone, my wife said that the atmosphere of the office changed dramatically," Felps said. "People started helping each other, playing classical music on their radios, and going out for drinks

after work. But when he returned to the office, things returned to the unpleasant way they were."[97]

The three categories of behavior that Felps attributes to bad apples map directly onto the Big Five facets of conscientiousness, agreeableness, and neuroticism, which, as we discussed earlier, were shown from the work of Barrick and Mount to predict overall team performance.

Although a limited body of research addresses the characteristics of objectionable team members, almost no studies focus on defining the attributes of effective team members. On the other hand, plain old experience and expert opinion (as distinct from research) abounds.

My colleagues, Tomas Chamorro-Premuzic, Robert Hogan, and Rob Kaiser, outline these truisms in a paper concerning employability.[98] They observe that although high IQ is often associated with work success, many bright individuals either fail their selection interviews or lack the interpersonal skills needed to sustain employment. Like Felps, Chamorro-Premuzic et al. note that unemployable people are irritable, challenging, and quarrelsome; or they display bad judgment; or they will be stubborn, non-conforming, and insubordinate

The essential question is: What determines a potentially good worker (and team member)? The answer lies in three broad maxims (see Figure 12): be competent (able), be kind (rewarding), and work hard (willing).

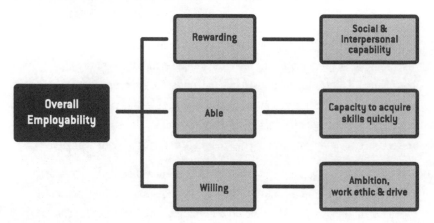

Figure 12. The RAW Model of Employability

Earvin "Magic" Johnson, the renowned Los Angeles Lakers basketball player, high-lighted the rewarding component of the model when he paraphrased JFK: "Ask not what your teammates can do for you, but what you can do for your teammates." Being a good teammate starts from subjugating one's personal desires to the needs of the team.

The model of employability depicted in Figure 12 easily maps onto the Big Five model, and it can be tested. As we saw above, the more team members who score high on the Big Five attribute of agreeableness, the better the team performs.[99] In addition, the presence of emotionally stable *and* agreeable team members (or re-warding, in the model above) improves cohesion and team performance, particu-larly when the work is pressured, stressful, or emotionally intense.[100]

Similarly, research findings report that teams with high average scores on open-ness (which forms part of the able component) perform better in changing or uncertain situations. For example, one study used a computerized simulation in which a critical communication link disappeared halfway through the task, forc-ing teams to modify and adapt to successfully complete the task.[101] In the face of the breakdown, team member openness and drive were associated with flexibility and, subsequently, higher task achievement. In contrast, being rule bound, which is the dark side of high scores on conscientiousness, was negatively related to both adaptability and task achievement.

One further study has shown team learning to be positively linked to openness,[102] especially when the team is diverse in terms of gender, experience, or skills. Individ-uals high on openness tend to adopt a more receptive approach to dissimilar oth-ers, thus encouraging information elaboration and, as a result, better performance.

The last factor that Chamorro-Premuzic, Hogan, and Kaiser point to concerns con-scientiousness. As we saw earlier, teams whose members score uniformly high on conscientiousness tend to commit to high levels of performance goals, effort, and planning.

Here's how the All-Star NBA player Kevin Love made the same points:

Figure 13. The Team Is Bigger Than You

Those of you who know Champ will appreciate this... I'd like to tribute the best teammate I've ever had. James Jones aka Champ. You taught me more than you know the past 2 years—what it takes to win, how to be a better teammate, how to balance the good/bad off the court, and most importantly... putting team first. Sacrifice for the better of the team, and in order to lead sometimes you have to learn how to follow. You've been to 6 straight Finals. You've been the constant presence we needed in the locker room. You're the ultimate work horse. The lessons you taught me will stay with me for the rest of my career and life after basketball. No one can avoid the ups and downs of the Playoffs, and when many wrote me off after a tough stretch in the Finals... you and the team stuck by me allowing me to flourish and make plays when it mattered.

▬ Kevin Love

USING PERSONALITY TO COMPOSE TEAMS

*Humans are the most dangerous, consequential things on
the planet. Shouldn't we know something about them?*

— *Robert Hogan*

It is the way of science to pick through conflicting data. Suzanne Bell's 2007 review revealed some inconsistent results in that the same personality attribute—like extraversion—may exert positive effects on team performance in some settings but degrade performance in others. Psychology is especially prone to saying, "it depends" because our techniques show relationships more than they show causation. So, here's a quick primer, and we can use the example of why iPhones cause deaths from falling down stairs. The figure below shows this relationship clearly:

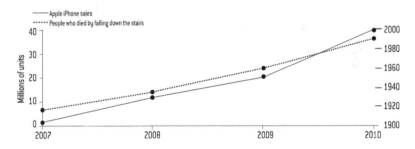

Figure 14. Stair-Fall Deaths and iPhone Sales Growth http://tylervigen.com/view_correlation?id=28669

It's clear that as iPhone sales go up, so do the number of people dying from falling down stairs. Is it because they are consumed by the urge to look at their new phones and stumble? Perhaps. But probably not. Rather, the relation between iPhones and tumbles is just a *spurious* correlation. Or in other words, it's a coincidence.

To cope with weird findings like that, social science research developed a rule of thumb called the specificity-matching principle. It was developed to account for the fact that outcomes in naturally occurring settings, like teamwork, are affected by many factors and not just the variables that a researcher is studying. The specificity-matching principle tells us to match variables sensibly—the closer the logical connection, the better.

This principle says iPhone sales might logically predict stock price rather than deaths through stair falls. You can see this relationship below:

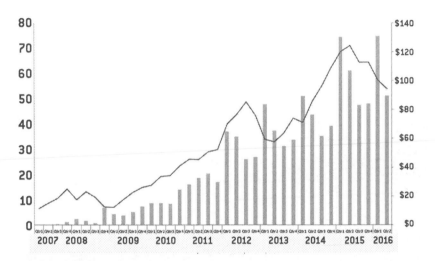

Figure 15. A Better Correlation

iPhone sales correlate positively with Apple's stock price. And, logically, it's a sensible relationship.

It's the same with personality and teams. We see links sometimes and not at other times. But logically, it makes sense that how people behave and relate should impact team performance. We also expect team success to be affected by things besides personality, like the caliber of the team members' skills and training, the competence of the team leader, the state of the team's resources, and the support provided inside the firm. Amidst all of that noise, the fact that we observe frequent relationships between personality and teams alerts us that we are studying a powerful mechanism.

How does personality impact teamwork, then? A recent paper by team researcher Jeffery LePine sketched two pathways through which personality affects team performance.[103] One path leads directly from personality to team performance via individual behavior. A bad-apple teammate who soured trust so much it degraded the team's performance would constitute an example of this path.

The other path is through the impact of personality on processes. As LePine described it:

> [This path addresses] members' interdependent acts that convert inputs into outcomes through cognitive, verbal, and behavioral activities directed toward organizing task work to achieve collective goals. These processes are differentiated from emergent states, which describe cognitive, motivational, and affective states of teams, rather than the nature of team members' interaction.[104]

LePine is saying that if ill-disciplined introverts comprised the entire team, the team would be likely to fail at establishing a shared direction with clear deliverables because they wouldn't interact with one another. (There is a case study documenting exactly this point below.)

Three broad sets of activities qualify as team processes:

1. Planning and measurement activities that guide the team towards task accomplishment, such as asking, "What are our goals?" and "How will we know we've been successful?"
2. Action processes that occur when the team is engaging in behaviors, like coordinating and delivering technical work, that lead directly to goal achievement.
3. Interpersonal processes, like coping with conflict, generating cohesion, and handling emotions, used to manage relationships within the team.

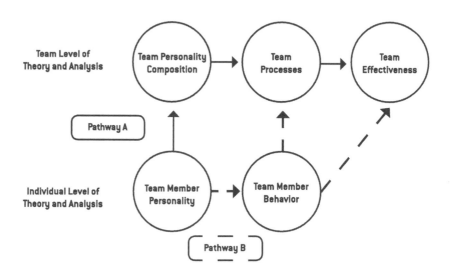

Figure 16. Team Processes Moderate the Link Between Personality and Team Performance

LePine concluded that who you are drives how you act, which affects what the team does. And what the team does impacts how effective the team will be.

COLLECTIVE TEAM PERSONALITY

This is an important point. LePine's model suggests that behavior on the team is a function of personality in aggregate and of individuals' personalities, so using personality to construct compatible work teams is a reasonable way to get good performance.

Another line of work highlighting the importance of collective personality to team performance is to consider what researchers have termed *team intelligence*.[105] In this context, intelligence is not the same as being smart. Rather, researchers have found that the ability of the team as a whole to think about its strategy and thus improve its performance has accounted for close to a third of the difference between high-performing and low-performing teams. A team of high-IQ geniuses will not out-perform a team with average IQs if the geniuses tend to be weak in understanding their colleagues' intentions and needs.

Nancy Cooke from the Human Systems Engineering School in Arizona describes team intelligence as follows:

> Teams... are capable of cognition. They make decisions as a unit, as in the case of the Yarnell Hill firefighters who for unknown reasons decided in June 2013 to leave a safe burned area and head to another [area] through unburned brush, where they became trapped by the fire [and died].... But where does team cognition reside?[106]

Team intelligence is an emergent phenomenon, derived from the interactions between team members as they share information about their environment and context, form plans, share tasks, and make decisions (embodied in LePine's processes above). Importantly, this idea coincides with the findings of the earlier-reviewed MIT Media Lab studies, which showed that teams who engaged with each other outperformed teams that were uncommunicative.

And what drives team intelligence and the frequency of a team's interactions? The best predictor was social perceptiveness, measured in this study by a test known as Reading the Mind in the Eyes Test. The test (you can take it here: http://nyti.ms/2vqBHSW) measures people's ability to judge others' emotional states from looking only at pictures of their eyes. Research has shown that focusing on and understanding the mental states of others is central to agreeableness.[107]

PERSONALITY IS ADDITIVE

The discussion above suggests that personality is additive at the team level. That is, would increasing the number of conscientious team members improve team performance?

The answer to that question is, for the most part, yes. One of the most robust findings in team research is that including more conscientious people on a team boosts performance. For example, a Swedish study of army-tank crews found that the least conscientious member's score predicted performance. The lower the score, the worse the tank crew did; the higher that member's score, the better the crew did.

But remember our caveat earlier, that contradictory findings abound in psychology. John Hollenbeck and Stephen Humphrey showed that too high or too low extraversion scores were both associated with less effective performance when compared to a team with a mix of high and low-scoring extraverts (i.e., high variability in the team scores).[108]

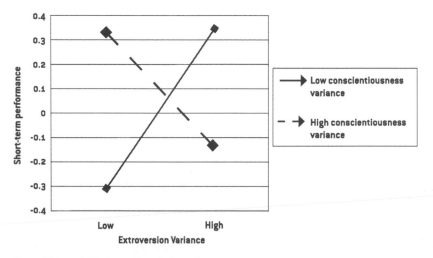

Figure 17. Conscientiousness Counts, Sometimes

The teams that delivered the best performances primarily comprised both high-conscientiousness members *and* a mix of introverts and extroverts.

The important point is that when it comes to personality, a mix of personalities seems to deliver better results. Loading a team with conscientious people is not a recipe for success in all cases. As with extraversion, too much of a good thing can generate poor outcomes. A team composed of too many rule-following, disciplined members may suppress those who offer alternative viewpoints.[109]

Matthew Prewett and his colleagues at the University of Florida reached a similar conclusion to LePine's, with an important addition: a team's collective personality will wield a stronger and more direct influence on team behaviors and processes (see Figure 16) than it does on team results, per se.[110] That is, performance is affected mostly by how people act and behave on the team.

Another important point is that personality composition becomes more important to overall team performance as the degree of interdependence required increases.

In other words, the more teamwork the task requires, like basketball, the more the team's composite personality affects team functioning and performance.

So, we might try to answer the question posed earlier about the composition of the crew on the three-year space voyage to Mars: what is the ideal mix of personalities? Elon Musk needs a team that:

1. Has all calm, stable and resilient members.
2. Has a mix of extroverts and introverts, but not too high or too low.
3. Has more high- than low-agreeable members, who can foster trust and care for each other.
4. Has more high-conscientious people than low.
5. Holds some important values in common.

THE POWER OF VALUES

Ahh, values. If personality is the surface manifestation of our character, then values are the deep roots of our behavior and preferences. Shared values bind; divergent values conflict.

To restate an earlier point, war and conflict between groups fundamentally drove team-based psychology. One of the most important questions to ask was, "Are these people on my team or not?" That question means that human beings are programmed to look for differences and similarities when encountering others for the first time. When we look for similarities or differences, we look first at surface-level indicators like skin color, clothing, or sexual orientation. We categorize others on the basis of looks all the time, even though this can lead to misjudgments and conflict.

> ... the more teamwork the task requires, like basketball, the more the team's composite personality affects team functioning and performance.

In fact, relationship conflicts in teams crop up more where there are obvious visible differences between members than through differences in any other demographic characteristics.[111] While task conflict is useful for team performance because it can lead to new ideas and creative solutions, relationship conflict diverts team members from the mission by reducing trust and increasing the time that leaders spend resolving interpersonal disputes.

To illustrate, imagine that Sarah, a young designer, is selected to serve on a prestigious project team charged with creating a new consumer product. In fact, the project is so important that the company has flown the new team to an exclusive resort for a week of inauguration and planning. As Sarah takes her place at the table, she begins to inspect her colleagues. The team seems very different to her: for one thing, she is the youngest person in the room. Additionally, the team includes people from around the world, and, from what Sarah is hearing, English isn't everyone's first language. She can sense everyone's nervousness, and surmises that the whole team has the same question: will we all get along well enough to make the project succeed?

> Values act as the superglue that connects people in teams.

Finding a way for the team to surmount surface-level differences and unite without relationship conflict would be ideal. Nature should invent a psychological glue for teams.

Well, it has. Values act as the superglue that connects people in teams.

CHOICE, PURPOSE, AND IDENTITY

Values act as a compass to point us in a particular direction when faced with choices. For example, a team collects a small windfall in an office sweepstakes. When they gather to talk about what to do with the $200, some people want to use the money for drinks and socializing, while others want to give it to charity. Instantly, two groups form: values are shaping our preferences and directing individuals towards certain types of people and away from others.

For the most part, values are unconscious. People notice values more when they are faced with a decision or a choice that isn't easy to make. That situation occurred to the US Olympic swimmer Ryan Lochte, whose story of being robbed at gunpoint at the Rio Olympics in 2016 turned out to be a cover-up for his own drunken antics at a gas station. Citing incompatibility with their values, many of his sponsors subsequently dropped their endorsements because, in the words of Speedo:

Figure 18. Speedo Declares Its Values

Thus, values can promote either group alignment or group disagreement, depending on whether team members' values are aligned or at odds. But here's the rub: because values are frequently unconscious, team members act from assumptions. It's only when the team confronts difficult choices that value differences are exposed. Operating from assumptions is operating blind; without values on the table, consensus and collaboration are harder to achieve.

When a team's values are similar, priorities are easier to agree on, and the team feels closer, often without recognizing why. People search for environments that are compatible with their interests and values, and in matching environments they achieve better performance, more persistence, and more satisfaction.[112] Conversely, members whose values fail to match the shared set held by others are more likely to leave the team.[113]

In 2007, I conducted research into a dozen or so senior-leadership teams. One of the key differences between high- and low-performing teams was whether the team had shared values or not (we came to call shared values "anchors"). Higher-performing teams that exhibited one or more value anchors displayed stronger task and social cohesion than did their lower-performing counterparts. In interviews with the anchored teams, I was impressed by the way team members talked about their ease in making difficult decisions, even though they debated issues vigorously. In contrast, leaders of the unmoored teams described being confused by the way simple conflicts seemed to get the team stuck, blocked, and antagonistic.

This finding intrigued me so much that I pored over the sparse literature on values diversity. To my delight, a fairly clear consensus, showing that shared values do indeed improve team performance, emerged from the research. A typical finding came from a recent study of sixty teams whose mission was to complete a manual task called the Chinese Bridge.[114] The task required each team to design and build a replica of a real bridge, using twenty rubber bands and thirty-three plastic pipes of three different sizes. The teams were obliged to use all of the materials. Although the researchers expected value diversity to enhance team performance. What they found, instead, was a link between values similarity and task performance and team cohesion. More diverse teams performed *less well*. In the teams with similar values, researchers also observed less conflict, as I had with the executive teams.

Shared values provide the foundation upon which team culture is formed—the sum of what individuals attract and appreciate. Over time, people create rules, norms, and standards that embody and embed shared group values, and this process, in turn, evolves into a shared culture. Lochte's sponsor Speedo rejected him because his behavior no longer fit with their values.

Shared team values affect teams in three main ways. First, they enable anchored teams to be more efficient because common values make decision-making easier and faster. The advantage of shared values is that when the members of a team with shared values orient themselves towards the goals, tasks, and behaviors that matter most to them, they are orienting themselves to the *same* goals, tasks, and behaviors. On the other hand, as the bridge-building teams above demonstrated, values diversity makes agreement more difficult and can engender disagreement about which task elements are critical to success. Moreover, anchored teams are more likely to create trust, which allows conflicts to be handled productively.[115] In contrast, unmoored teams will exhibit low cohesion and take longer to develop trusting bonds, driving up transaction costs and slowing decision-making.

The second way congruent values are essential in creating high-performing teams is via team development. With a shared value base, teams improve faster, omitting the long, often stormy, phase that can precede reaching effective performance.[116]

> More stable teams outperformed the less stable teams.

For example, the core members of the Cali drug cartel held the same values of innovation and commerciality.[117] Although the cartel operated at the same time as Pablo Escobar's Medellin cartel, the Cali cartel functioned as a team of teams. They became known for their innovative supply chains (at one stage, establishing a distribution center in New York) and for their financial acumen (accruing legitimate investments in commercial companies). Because they shared similar backgrounds (well-born Colombians) and held similar values, the members of the Cali cartel implemented new ideas faster than the Medellin cartel.

The third way shared values improve teamwork is through boosting the stability of the team. Teams who remain together develop strong connections and commitments to each other. Individuals who adopt a long-term perspective regarding their team membership are more likely than short-term thinkers to put team interests above their own. An absence of shared values decreases members' satisfaction with and commitment to their team, while increasing their determination to leave.[118]

Actually, the sports world has demonstrated the benefits of team stability very well. Mark van Vught, a Dutch psychologist, investigated the relation between performance and player turnover in the English and Italian football (soccer) leagues.[119] The more stable teams outperformed the less stable teams on a wide range of performance indicators, including the league ranking, the aggregate points scored, and the number of goals conceded.

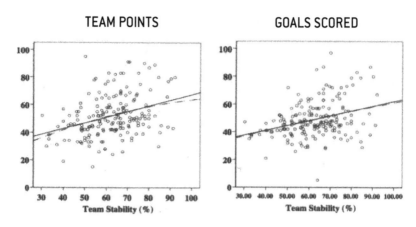

Figure 19. Stable Teams Score More Often

Van Vught concluded that these effects could not be attributed to other factors, such as a team's wealth or past performance, the average length of its contracts, or the average age of its players. Stable teams tend to perform better. The team's ability to coordinate itself increases as it spends more time together and develops a shared knowledge base of team processes. Conversely, high turnover disrupts a team's ability to draw upon a shared memory of what to do.

In conclusion, the lesson of values is clear: people who share similar beliefs about what is important and valuable at work and in life will bond more quickly, experience healthier conflict, and be more attuned to each other's needs. Common values are an excellent glue for holding teams together.

FAULTLINES

Anyone who has been in a relationship might recall the early days and weeks with their newfound love. At the start of a relationship, most people monitor their behavior to present themselves in the best possible light, showing their brighter side. One might pay more attention to one's table manners, sit up straighter, or make additional effort to join in conversations. Almost everyone takes extra care over his or her appearance.

Most people will also make an effort to suppress behaviors they think might upset or annoy the other person. No matter how hard we work, as the relationship continues, partners are likely to see more of the *dark side*—that set of unconscious or defensive interpersonal habits that aggravate others.[120] Dark-side personality traits are a person's potential path to derail, to run off the tracks, and crash. They emerge when people are no longer careful about managing how others view them. That might be because they are stressed, irritable, tired, hungry, drunk, stoned, or indifferent to their effect on others. As a result, a new lover's fascinating confidence and positivity on a first date might, after repeated exposure, morph into a charmless play for the limelight and a Pollyanna-like outlook on life. Or perhaps the endearing caution and concern displayed on the first few dates subsequently looks like a controlling, anxious timidity.

Dark-side tendencies rest on flawed assumptions about how to advance one's agenda. Robert Kaiser has noted that these dark tendencies are tied to the bright side of one's personality in a twisted knot of strengths and weaknesses.[121] For instance, passion can be tied to emotional volatility or violence; confidence can be entwined with arrogance; eagerness to please can be tangled around an inability to think for oneself. It's hard work. Although we all want our partner to be warm and approachable, concerned about others, and so on, we also want them to censor their dark sides as much as humanly possible without *acting*—that'd be horrible.

This twisted knot of strengths and weaknesses impacts teams, too. For example, a few years ago I conducted research on the characteristics of people who apply for chief executive roles. The results showed that the personality feature they held in common and that most distinguished them from other people, was a psychological trait called ambition: being competitive, energetic, achievement-oriented and self-confident.[122] Recall Kaiser's point that strengths are tangled with weaknesses: people who score high on ambition tend to be seen by others as leader-like. Yet the dark side of competitiveness and self-confidence is arrogance, narcissism, and an inability to listen. Having to work with a whole team of these people can be unpleasant.

At their best, teams composed of highly ambitious members move quickly and set big goals. But the dark side of a room filled with competitive fast-movers often means a cascade of goals, urgent demands, competing agendas, and too many people speaking at once.

And what happens if some in the team are strongly ambitious and goal driven, whereas others are cautious, careful, and concerned with detail? That composition represents a team *faultline*—a potential for the team to split into cliques—that might manifest in a way similar to a faultline in a real executive team.

When a new CEO took over the reins of SciX, a global supplier of science and health products, the board gave him a mandate to grow the business aggressively. After all, the company's treasure trove of patents and deep bench of scientists were the envy of its global competition. Furthermore, SciX had recently changed its capital structure and had accumulated a war chest for investment. The CEO carefully reviewed the existing leadership team and winnowed it from an unmanageable 15 to a more useful group of eight, hiring talent from top international competitors to complement the existing members.

Up to this point, science had strongly led the business. The CEO's new team retained a science and operations representation, with five of the eight having a combined company history of nearly 100 years. However, the new talent (and the CEO) differed considerably from those with long tenure; they were brash, outgoing, ambitious, and staunchly commercial. At meetings, they swapped business cases from top schools, like INSEAD and Wharton, and bandied phrases reminiscent of the tech industry, like "fail fast" and "we need to find blue oceans." Reports from independent reviews convinced the team that the company could organically grow by about a third, and, with acquisitions, possibly double its revenues.

The new team members also encouraged more openness and debate in meetings than the long-time employees were used to, but the change was refreshing. The atmosphere was positive, tough, and relentless. Everyone enjoyed the new focus on data and measurement, and the team aligned behind the new CEO.

By the five-month mark, though, the sunny start had grown cloudy. The newer members dominated meetings and produced goals, metrics, plans, and targets for the organization. As aggressive as ever, they criticized the speed at which the company innovated, demanded expense cuts to improve their margins, planned a big reorganization, and were impatient with delays caused by ambitious IT projects. While the new crew seemed to build on one another, feeding off their combined energy and pushing each other to be more aggressive, the longer-tenured employees felt that their wisdom and challenges went unheeded. Although, individually, their plans were rational, when combined, the plans were proving impossible for the business to execute.

Psychologically speaking, these dark-side behaviors (which we call derailers) have useful antecedents; they help people manage the stress of difficult situations. Trying to prove themselves in their new positions, the brash, risky, talkative members of the SciX team displayed the very characteristics that the CEO found attractive. But sharing such similar derailers amplified their effect in the team. A faultline emerged because the more brash they became, the more the older team members withdrew (which was their dark-side response).

Left unchecked or unnoticed, derailers can interfere with the ability to build relationships and maintain a cohesive, goal-oriented team. Because members' moods and feelings are contagious, the effect will flow through to the broader team.[123] So it proved at SciX. Six months into his tenure, the CEO got a call from the chairman, warning him that the board had noticed a split emerging in the team and that they wanted it healed.

Faultlines and shared derailers lead to three broad effects. The first is shared blind spots. To use the Bay of Pigs example, Kennedy's cabinet shared their young president's self-confidence and arrogant conviction about American military superiority, a blind spot that caused them to discount the possibility of failure. And in the SciX situation, the leadership crew fell victim to their own hubris and blind to the impact of their behavior. In doing so, they approached the brink of their own disaster by ignoring and alienating their colleagues.

The second, and related, effect is multiplication. Multiplication occurs when derailing behaviors trigger similar responses from others, leading to a cascade of deeply destructive patterns that damage the team and sap productivity.

For example, on a $400 million road construction project I worked on, one of the mission-critical elements was to build the dozens of concrete piers that would carry bridges. Typically, outside contractors perform this highly specialized task. Nevertheless, as a calculated risk, the leadership had opted to do the work in-house and appointed a promising young engineer to lead the work. Although technically capable, he was inexperienced and so relied heavily on his team of experienced foremen and leading hands. Against a deadline, fighting bad weather, slow steel shipments, and delays with engineering designs, the bridge pier team was behind schedule almost from the start. Under normal conditions, engineers are detail-oriented perfectionists. Now, faced with time pressure and becoming stressed, the team began to micromanage every aspect of the job, working longer and longer hours, constructing ultra-detailed plans, and overseeing each aspect of the task. The more they planned, the less they got done, and the tighter they managed each step of the process, including telling tough, experienced construction workers how to execute simple tasks. Ultimately, the delays and the skilled hands' blunt-spoken rebellion led to confrontations, and the young project manager was removed. Like a boulder rolling down a hill, once multiplication effects begin they can be hard to stop. Insight and awareness are essential to help teams mitigate these risks.

The third and final impact of shared dark-side derailers is competitive responding. Team members whose dark-side personalities exacerbate one another can trigger a kind of arms race of derailment by increasingly responding in the very manner that triggers further dark-side behavior.

In 2010, playing in the FIFA World Cup tournament in South Africa, the French team disintegrated when the players went on strike in protest of their coach. The football world was shocked when they exited the tournament in the minor rounds.

France's team had been dogged by clashes between players and coaches before the tournament began. Matters came to a head when the coach, Raymond Domenech, sent striker Nicolas Anelka—nicknamed "Le Sulk" because of his attitude—back to France after a half-time row during the game against Mexico. Anelka reportedly told his coach to "fuck off, you dirty son of a whore."

The French team refused to train once Anelka had been sent home, and captain Patrice Evra had such a heated fight with the fitness coach, Robert Duverne, that they had to be physically separated by Domenech. The team refused to practice, walked off the training pitch, went to their bus, closed the curtains, and delivered to Coach Domenech a letter to be read to the press:

> All the players without exception want to declare their opposition to the decision taken by the FFF to exclude Nicolas Anelka from the squad...At the request of the squad, the player in question attempted

to have dialogue but his approach was ignored. The French Football Federation has at no time tried to protect the squad. . . .

At that point, the team manager, Jean-Louis Valentin, resigned and returned to France, saying, "They don't want to train. It's unacceptable. As for me, it's over. I'm leaving the federation. I'm sickened and disgusted." In their final game against South Africa, the French team played so badly that their own fans cheered for the opposition, who ultimately won. The dark side truly derailed the team.

"Faultlines" is a term borrowed from geology, referring to fractures or breaks in the underlying surface of the world. A faultline can be active and obvious to all, like in the example above, or dormant, existing, but not yet perceived.[124] The city of Christchurch had no known geographical faultlines. Yet when one appeared, the world was never the same for many of its citizens.

Dormant faultlines can be triggered by an event or a series of events. Presumably, the French football team all started their journey to the World Cup with hope in their hearts and the best of intentions. Yet personal differences, ambitions, and concerns about the coach's competence created the conditions for the catastrophic rift when Anelka was sent home.

Another important finding in recent research is that detecting a faultline and assessing its size is now possible.[125] One method of doing so is the Hogan Team Report, discussed below.

Faultlines are more likely to create problems when strong similarities exist among members *within* each subgroup, or large perceived differences exist *between* the subgroups. Similarities may be obvious, with regard to surface-level differences, like age, gender or skin color, but likenesses also extend to experience differences, geographic differences, and of course, psychological differences.

Recent work shows that faultlines, once apparent, tend to polarize group social networks. In practice, this situation results in team members' beginning to spend their time with like-minded individuals and avoiding people whom they perceive as dissimilar. In response, team members start to perceive groups with whom they are not affiliated as forming cliques or acting standoffish. This negative progression can be stopped and faultlines healed by using the following suggestions:

1. Create a mission and purpose so powerful that it transcends individuals' selfish interests and desires, at least for a period of time. How the French squandered such a powerful *raison d'etre* as playing for their country and winning a world tournament for the team is astonishing. *Sacre bleu!*

2. Build a psychologically safe environment that accepts disagreement and debate and views it as healthy. And *never allow the team to descend into personal attacks*. When team members are open to challenge and learn to appreciate and value the experiences and perspectives of others, the team will flourish. Moreover, the skills of dialogue are trainable.

3. Encourage cross-training.[126] Players who can span divides and build relationships are like gold to a team. These people are more likely to be psychologically agreeable or *relationship players*. They will be good listeners who want to sustain or nurture connections among others.

4. Encourage interactions. The MIT research that suggested that more interaction is better than less is relevant here. Design opportunities to connect parts of the team's workflow deep into the team norms. For the introverts, interactions can comprise emails, small gatherings, and sometimes, just being present.

Finally, don't select bad apples onto the team. And if you have some, get them off the team as soon as possible.

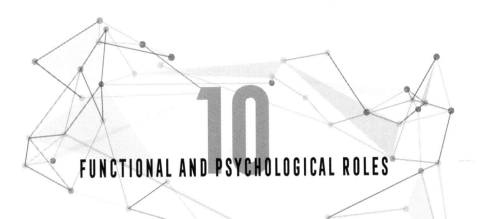

10

FUNCTIONAL AND PSYCHOLOGICAL ROLES

Here's a thought experiment: to create the best football team in the world, hire only players who are superbly fit, strong, and possess an indomitable will to win. No brainer, right?

Will this strategy reflect a winning formula?

It won't if the selections consist solely of fit, strong, and indomitable goalkeepers. Selecting players who are strong, doughty, and skilled for the functions required on the team (striker, wing, defender, and so on) is closer to a winning strategy.

Functional roles are analogous to the job descriptions found in many workplaces. An operating theatre, for example, requires a scrub nurse, a circulating tech, a surgeon, and an anesthesiologist. Yet as we've seen above, there is more to a successful team than just functional-role capability: people occupy psychological roles in a team as well. Swapping one equally competent striker for another will not produce the same result.

To Henry Ford's distress, people aren't empty organic machines that can be exchanged one for another. They come with hopes, fears, personalities, and histories, and if there are two equally skilled people to choose from, it's smarter to go for the one whose attributes and character will most contribute to the team. Character differences among individuals matter as much to a team's life as their technical skills do. Personality preferences carry significant consequences for the team's functioning and performance.

In the real world, functionally skilled teams fail because they lack people who can play important psychological roles. Here's a true case history of a technically competent team who nonetheless failed:

The Pacific Environmental Sustainability Agency[127] (ESA) is an Australian federal body that maintains a substantial estate of parks and wild ecological zones. Although principled, the agency had nevertheless acquired a reputation as earnest, rigid, righteous, and staffed by naive zealots. This reputation hurt its cause with the government: successive administrations cut nearly 30% of its baseline funding between 2008 and 2015. They wanted the ESA to become more entrepreneurial: "Generate returns from your parks," it was told. "Work with tourist operators to help fund your activities."

This message was anathema to the ESA, but to survive as a viable organization, it had to institute fundamental change. A three-phase plan called for co-funding conservation programs with chosen corporate sponsors, cutting non-core programs and staff numbers, and embedding a commercial and fiscally disciplined culture.

The finance division was the key player for the last component of the plan. They had to build new financial management tools, train and support line managers, and educate front-line staff on the more commercial approach. The finance director not only helped develop the plan, but was exceptionally supportive; everyone could see that he worked diligently for the cause. In addition, the accountants and financial specialists were all technically capable.

However, over the next six months, the finance director and his team missed deadlines, didn't connect to the line managers, and provided none of the commercial training and support that the turnaround plan called for.

When a team has a clear mission, support, and technically capable members and still fails, the failure is most likely an inability to get the softer side of its house in order. The team lacked people who could generate ideas, build relationships, or empathize with the line managers. These are all *psychological roles*.

MOTIVATING BEHAVIOR: FUNCTIONAL VS. PSYCHOLOGICAL ROLES

FUNCTIONAL ROLES

Does the *functional role* one occupies—accountant, receptionist, center forward, or lead singer—account for one's behavior towards other people on a team? People who don police uniforms tend to adopt behavior consistent with that role, and, when pulled over for speeding, most drivers will adopt the penitent role of the chastened guilty.

The logical extension of this idea suggests that lead singers of rock and roll bands are transformed by their role into drug-addled, self-promoting, over-sexed, and capricious narcissists; those who are required to deal with them (fellow band members, lawyers, accountant, groupies, roadies, and fans) collude and support them in that role because they get payoffs for doing so. The movie *Almost Famous*, about a 15-year-old budding music journalist touring with a wild rock band, is a good illustration of the effect that playing a role can have on a person.

But playing a role cannot be the whole story. Although roles shape and limit our actions, they are not the primary drivers of behavior. But a famous experiment designed to prove the opposite, that roles *do* govern behavior, observed the results it sought. The 1971 Stanford Prison Experiment, conducted by well-known psychologist Philip Zimbardo, arbitrarily selected male university students to assume the role of guard or prisoner.[128] The prisoners were picked up from their homes by real policemen, charged, fingerprinted, photographed, and then blindfolded and transported to a fake prison in the basement of Stanford University. As Zimbardo had expected, the guards adopted an authoritarian stance, doled out harsh punishments, and degraded the prisoners. In turn, the prisoners became passive and compliant, even to the point of harassing each other at the request of the guards. Originally scheduled to run eight days, two prisoners asked to leave early, and, out of concern for the other participants, the experiment was terminated after six days.

However, attempts to replicate the experiment by two British psychologists produced very different results from Zimbardo's.[129] Examining the original results, along with the original study documents, including films, showed that Zimbardo had unwittingly given instructions and coaching that told the participants how they should behave. Rather than roles' driving behavior, the replication concluded that roles exerted only a small effect on the observed conduct.

The best explanation is that roles and personality interact to produce behavior. For instance, the police are generally constrained in ways that fit their role in society and the powers society delegates to them. Nevertheless, although the largest percentage within the population of police officers will be rule-abiding and helpful, a small percentage will be domineering and violent, and some smaller percentage will be corrupt.

Or reconsider rock stars. Lead singers' role in rock and roll bands gives them license to behave as indulgent, narcissistic, rule-defying anti-heroes to teenagers. If the job description reads "lots of money, parties, free sex, constant adulation, touring, and normal rules don't apply" it will attract certain kinds of people and repel others. And even then, not all lead singers are narcissistic, licentious hedonists.

As discussed earlier, one's personality determines how one behaves within the boundaries of a role. Sir Mick Jagger may well have had many relationships and fathered children by multiple women, whether or not he was the lead singer of the Rolling Stones. Being fabulously wealthy, perpetually on television, and often on tour no doubt helped.

Or consider a role for which no real training exists and no particular skill set is compulsory: the President of the United States. Presidents have most frequently had law degrees, but farmers, businessmen, soldiers, and even one actor have all served as president. For this job, what matters more than one's professional role is character. If character didn't matter, then the person who occupies the White House would be irrelevant: Bill Clinton would have performed the role in the same way George Bush, Barack Obama, or Ulysses S. Grant did. But American voters certainly don't believe all presidents perform their role the same way; they base their judgments about presidential aptitude on their perceptions of the character and personality of those who seek office.

PSYCHOLOGICAL ROLES

Anyone who has worked on a team understands that people contribute to the psychological life of the team in different ways and that each way is determined by personality. Some people are sociable and help smooth the interactions and dynamics of the group. If they are also energetic, then they are likely to organize meetings, get-togethers, and beers after work. Other people are results-oriented drivers who set high standards, are disappointed by losses, and are more keen to finish the task than go to the pub.

Paul Maritz, the one-time CEO of software company VMware, describes team roles like this:

> At the risk of oversimplifying, I think that in any great leadership team, you find at least four personalities, and you never find [them] in a single person. You need to have somebody who is a strategist or visionary, who sets the goals for where the organization needs to go. You need to have somebody who is the classic manager . . . making sure that everybody knows what they need to do and making sure that tasks are broken up into manageable actions. You need a champion for the customer . . . who empathizes and understands how customers will see it. Then, lastly, you need the enforcer. You need somebody who says, "We've stared at this issue long enough . . . We're going to do something about it."[130]

People intuitively know that diversity is useful on a team. They also understand that personality is what creates the diversity in how people act and behave in the group.

Psychologists and those who ponder management have made many attempts to describe the psychological roles that people play on a team. Two of the most popular efforts have been the Belbin Team Role Inventory and the Myers-Briggs Type Indicator. Both aim to help teammates understand each other and put their own and others' behavior in context.

I dislike both these tools. They rely on the unsophistication of consultants, managers, and HR departments and use an old trick, called the Barnum effect, to create anodyne descriptions of psychological role behavior.

The Barnum effect, named after the circus entrepreneur, P.T. Barnum, describes the credence people assign to vague but positive statements describing their personalities. Bertram R. Forer, a clinical psychologist, first noted the effect when he administered a personality test to a class and gave them written personality interpretations, which they then rated according to how accurately they believed the interpretation fit them.[131] Unbeknownst to the students, Forer gave every student the same description taken from an astrology book:

> People contribute to the psychological life of the team in different ways.

1. While you have some personality weaknesses, you are generally able to compensate for them.

2. Disciplined and self-controlled outside, you tend to be worrisome and insecure inside.

3. At times, you have serious doubts as to whether you have made the right decision or done the right thing.

4. You prefer a certain amount of change and variety and become dissatisfied when hemmed in by restrictions and limitations.

Students rated the descriptions as highly accurate. Sigh. How easily we are fooled by hucksterism. I review the MBTI and the Belbin below, to make the point that we can do much better.

Meredith Belbin, a professor at the Henley Management College in England, spent time watching small teams of management students interact on class projects. Noting that some people tended to be idea generators, whereas others were good at following through and making sure that the team finished its projects, he began to compile a list of team roles. His work became the Belbin Team Role Inventory, which describes nine roles:

TABLE 4. BELBIN'S TEAM TYPES

Implementer	Well-organized and predictable. Takes basic ideas and makes them work in practice. Can be slow.
Shaper	Lots of energy and action, challenging others to move forwards. Can be insensitive.
Completer/Finisher	Reliably sees things through to the end, ironing out the wrinkles and ensuring everything works well. Can worry too much and not trust others.
Plant	Solves difficult problems with original and creative ideas. Can be a poor communicator and may ignore the details.
Monitor/Evaluator	Sees the big picture. Thinks carefully and accurately about things. May lack energy or ability to inspire others.
Specialist	Has expert knowledge/skills in key areas and will solve many problems here. Can be disinterested in all other areas.
Coordinator	Respected leader who helps everyone focus on their task. Can be seen as excessively controlling.
Team Worker	Cares for individuals and the team. Good listener and works to resolve social problems. Can have problems making difficult decisions.
Resource/Investigator	Explores new ideas and possibilities with energy and with others. Good networker. Can be too optimistic and lose energy after the initial flush.

Belbin's work quickly gathered momentum in the British commercial world and remains in use today. Despite its commercial success, academic psychologists harshly criticized Belbin's work. Belbin had been consistently vague about his methods; in addition, he altered his role descriptions and even the number of roles he measured. The eminent British psychologist, Professor Adrian Furnham took Belbin to task for sloppy work, describing his role taxonomy as statistically weak and ill-considered. Subsequently, not only have critics maintained that Belbin described too many roles, but also that further study has shown that several of his role descriptions overlap. Furnham bemoaned the fact that:

> It is both interesting and annoying to . . . find that both consultants and clients seem uninterested and disinterested in validating theories and measures upon which they often make enormously important decisions. Even more perplexing is the fact that once measures have been shown to be seriously wanting, it has little or no effect on the popular use and retention of the measure.[132]

Belbin's work stimulated considerable interest in team roles. He popularized the notion that psychological roles differ from functional ones, and that people naturally fall into certain informal roles based on their personalities. (In fact, factor analysis studies have found that the Belbin team roles can be presented in terms of the Five Factor Model, and that Belbin was likely to have described the Big Five personality traits in his observations of the Henley teams).[133]

Of course, the granddaddy of all team-building inventories is the Myers-Briggs Type Indicator (MBTI). Isabel Briggs Myers and her mother, Katharine Briggs, developed the MBTI to operationalize Carl Jung's theory of types. Their goal was to identify an individual's basic preferences for each of four dichotomies implicit in Jung's philosophy (i.e., thinking [T] vs. feeling [F]; sensing [S] vs. intuition [N]; extraversion [E] vs. introversion [I]; judging [J] vs. perceiving [P]). People end up with a four-letter code made up of their preference for one or the other of those four scales:

ISTJ	ISFJ	INFJ	INTJ
ISTP	ISFP	INFP	INTP
ESTP	ESFP	ENFP	ENTP
ESTJ	ESFJ	ENFJ	ENTJ

Figure 20: The MBTI Type Table

The Myers-Briggs is the world's most popular psychological test. It has long been a staple of educational institutions, selection systems, and organizational workshops. As popular as the Myers-Briggs is, it has attracted some of the harshest criticism from scientists: "In social science, we use four standards: are the categories reliable, valid, independent, and comprehensive? For the MBTI, the evidence says not very, no, no, and not really."[134]

Critics raise two principal concerns about the MBTI. The first questions whether the dichotomies really exist. This point is important because the MBTI places people in mutually exclusive categories. However, the evidence supporting these categories is poor, leading one researcher to note that the scientific basis for dividing people into categories is nonexistent.[135] Further, MBTI respondents often react poorly to the all-or-nothing nature of the boxes:

> MBTI is the default training solution for any kind of team-building event ... People very often say something like, "Um, I think that I am not just a T or an F. Can I be somewhere in the middle?" And my colleagues will patiently explain that you must be one or the other. This is the most disputed aspect of the whole thing. And yet there we are explaining with complete authority that 'No, you ARE either a thinker or a feeler.' It is stupid.[136]

The second issue with the Myers-Briggs is that it doesn't describe how people actually behave. A number of reviews have shown that the MBTI is a poor predictor of on-the-job behavior and of career outcomes.[137] As Robert Hogan has noted, "Most personality psychologists regard the MBTI as little more than an elaborate fortune cookie."[138]

THE PROBLEM WITH EXISTING ROLE TOOLS

Although the insight that people play more than functional roles when they serve on a team is critically important, the Belbin Inventory, the MBTI, and other descriptions of team roles present four main problems. First, research has demonstrated that these tools do not adequately describe separate roles. That is, from a technical perspective, the questionnaires are scientifically flawed.[139] Second, tools that provide for seven, nine, or 16 different psychological roles operating on a single team have no basis in evidence. To show how senseless this trend is, consider that the website MindTools lists no fewer than 26 team roles:[140]

MINDTOOLS TEAM ROLES

1. Initiator/Contributor
2. Information Seeker
3. Information Giver
4. Opinion Seeker
5. Opinion Giver
6. Elaborator
7. Coordinator
8. Orienter [sic]
9. Evaluator/Critic
10. Energizer
11. Procedural Technician
12. Recorder
13. Encourager
14. Harmonizer
15. Compromiser
16. Gatekeeper/Expediter
17. Observer/Commentator
18. Follower
19. Aggressor
20. Blocker
21. Recognition Seeker
22. Self-Confessor
23. Disrupter/Playboy or Playgirl
24. Dominator
25. Help Seeker
26. Special Interest Pleader

An army of psychologists would have difficulty devising tests to capture the nuances these roles reflect, and some of the roles seem more like behaviors than personality characteristics.

The third point is that these types of tools aren't grounded in a modern understanding of personality. As we saw above, the Big Five has been remarkably useful in predicting a wide range of life outcomes, including promotions at work, safety behavior,[141] academic success, financial success, compliance with medical treatment,[142] and even long-term health outcomes.[143] And it is just as useful in understanding the roles people play on a team.

Finally, if one takes the view that a team can be more than the sum of its parts, then, logically, if individuals don't fit their functional or psychological roles, a team can be *less* than the sum of its parts, as well. If team members lack cohesiveness, or if their strong similarities blind them to their collective weaknesses, they risk failure.

Determining whether a team will be more or less than its individual members requires one to envision the team as a whole, which neither Belbin nor the MBTI can do. So, my colleagues and I set out to create a tool of our own.

11
THE HOGAN TEAM REPORT

The strength of the team is each individual member.
The strength of each member is the team.

— Phil Jackson

The beginning of this book explored the utility of teams from an evolutionary per-spective, considering them as a kind of super-weapon in ancient humans' fight for survival. Evolution shaped the human hardware and software that produces the emotional, behavioral, and physical aspects of cooperation. This evolution has enabled human beings to grasp the intentions of others, to read their emotions, and to mimic their behavior—and to do so exponentially better than apes, snakes, dogs, and termites can. In addition to what nature has provided, we also profit from the cultural wisdom and the encoded knowledge and technology, refined over thousands of generations. Modern humans have the best group-based operating system in history, a technology that, as Robert Hogan has pointed out, makes us the most dangerous and consequential species on the planet.

Nevertheless, we modern people are almost willfully blind to our shared talent, and we too rarely pay any conscious attention to teamwork. Explaining the hard aspects of team design that influence team performance, such as task type, team size, feedback, and leadership, seemed worthwhile, because they set the founda-tion for greatness.

Softer aspects of teamwork, like trust, cohesion, and fairness, also contribute to high performance, but are harder to influence directly. Instructing someone that they should trust the team is unlikely to prove successful. Rather, the softer el-ements of teamwork might be best thought of as arising from successfully en-gaging with the hard aspects of team functioning, as well as from having fair and competent leadership. Nonetheless, too few leaders give sufficient thought to or preparation for soft factors, like goals, norms, feedback, and measurement.

Finally, we surveyed the foundations of teams, which result from individual characteristics, like personality and values. These deep-level composition variables exert an impact on team performance principally through team processes and social cohesion, but their dark sides will emerge in the form of interpersonal problems. Personality variables affect team members' relationships and behavior, thereby producing a direct impact on overall team performance. Shared values both improve team trust and cooperation and exert an unconscious influence on decision-making.

With my colleague, Gus McIntosh, I wondered if we could do the same for the deep aspects of team functioning as the Rocket Model had done for the hard aspects, without succumbing to the problems that plague existing role tools like the Myers-Briggs. We were motivated to produce this report because, in our work coaching senior leadership teams, Gus and I had become aware of the interpersonal tension that often dominates these teams, but is never spoken about. We wanted to devise a way in which we could diagnose and visualize those dynamics and help a team see themselves as an entity, rather than as a set of one-on-one relationships.

Looking at the team as a whole is an important change in focus; most team building focuses on giving individual results to each person. This tactic tends to reward self-confident, competitive, and egotistical types who occupy senior positions in organizations. We also found that making sense of existing team tools, like the MBTI, is difficult because individual scores aggregated to the level of a team are difficult to interpret.

Making the team the unit of analysis helps team members learn to subsume their self-interest in deference to the team's needs, and instead, fosters a collective view of the team's strengths. It also promotes the team task by asking members to reflect on their collective suitability for the mission. Gus and I wanted to help teams look in the mirror and understand how their communal personality was likely to shape their performance.

Successful teams have an awareness of their composition and understand that a balance of personalities is important for effective performance. In contrast, unsuccessful teams seem unconscious, unseeing, or willfully ignorant of the impact of their different personalities, or they load up with people who are too similar. In short, a team's self-knowledge guides its development. Self-knowledge also helps individuals moderate their dark-side behavior.

PSYCHOLOGICAL ROLES

Formulating a team overview from the perspective of psychological roles was both novel and daunting. But we knew that the nine Belbin roles were too many. Other writers have suggested four as the correct number,[144] and some research has suggested three.[145]

To initiate our project, we began to start our team-performance coaching workshops by asking how many and what roles the participants thought that a team needs. Again and again, the attendees described four roles:

1. Someone to focus on results, getting things done, and being concerned with outcomes.
2. People who focus on team relations and inner harmony.
3. People who produce ideas and visions for the team.
4. Organizers, who ensure i's are dotted and t's crossed.

A few other role suggestions included people who play a hardheaded rationalist role and people who play a linking role.

We knew that, based on their personalities, people migrate to certain psychological roles within a team; in addition, certain personality styles constitute natural fit with certain psychological roles, as they do with particular functional roles. We settled on defining a set of five psychological roles that team members assume.

We used the Hogan Personality Inventory to guide our work. This instrument is one of the best-validated and most-researched personality tools available, and we were familiar with its developers. Consequently, we derived the roles algorithmically from the Hogan scales. The five roles are as follows:

Results. Team members who naturally focus on results tend to organize work, clarify roles, coordinate the team, and provide direction for others. They seek to guide work for others, are comfortable taking charge, and are active in attaining results. They tend to be socially self-confident, leader-like, competitive, and energetic. However, they may be overly competitive with their peers or subordinates and are not inclined to seek others' input.

Relationships. Team members who naturally focus on relationships are concerned about how team members feel and how well they get along. They are often upbeat, attuned to people's feelings, and accomplished at building cohesion and positive relationships. This role is defined by above-average results on both Extraversion and Agreeableness. Generally speaking, people who are average or high on these two factors are gregarious, outgoing, and talkative; others perceive them as being warm, friendly, approachable, and charming. They are perceptive, thoughtful, and cooperative team members who listen to others and foster trust and respect from peers and staff. However, they can be overly focused on others, prioritizing amicability over performance.

Process. Team members who naturally focus on process are concerned with implementation, the particulars of execution, and the use of process and systems to complete tasks. They are reliable, organized, and conscientious about following procedures, and attentive to details and implementation. They hold high standards for both their own and others' performance. However, others may view them as rigid and inflexible, people who don't appreciate the overall mission.

Innovation. Team members who naturally focus on innovation anticipate problems, recognize when conditions have changed, and know when the team needs to adapt. They spot trends and patterns quickly, enjoy solving problems, and generate creative solutions. Innovative role players are often imaginative, as well as creative, curious, and open-minded; they focus on the bigger picture and supply the team with a variety of ideas and solutions. However, they may have difficulty observing practicalities, preferring ideas and conceptualizing over implementation.

Pragmatism. Team members who naturally focus on pragmatism are practical, somewhat inflexible, challengers of ideas and theories. They promote realistic approaches and aren't easily swayed by the need to preserve harmony or innovation for their own sake. People who gravitate towards this role are level-headed, cautious in accepting new ideas, and favor a hands-on approach to solving problems. They are not easily swayed by emotions, and are comfortable confronting conflict. However, others may perceive them as ignoring both the overall mission and people's feelings.

To check our thinking, we worked with the research department at Hogan Assessment Systems (HAS) to simulate the distribution of our team roles against HAS's archive of psychological profiles. Importantly, the HAS archive comprised data for over 145,000 working adults who had completed the Hogan Personality Instrument (HPI) in 41 different languages. As a result, we were able to create language- and culture-free comparisons of individuals for each of the team roles. Table 5 shows the percentage of people who had played one of the five roles:

TABLE 5. THE DISTRIBUTION OF TEAM ROLES

DISTRIBUTION OF TEAM ROLES		
ROLE	N	%
Results	60,322	41.4%
Relationships	57,866	39.7%
Process	54,821	37.6%
Innovation	61,600	42.3%
Pragmatism	46,731	32.1%

The results above show that roughly 40% had played one of the roles. Conducting this analysis was important for establishing the spread of roles across a population. Hence, if we were to construct a team of 10 people chosen randomly from the 140,000 people in our archive, we should expect four individuals to assume the Results role, four to assume the Innovation role, and four to assume the Relationships role. We would expect slightly fewer to assume the Pragmatic role, but the difference wouldn't be large. The reason that the total of all the numbers in each role exceeded 10 is that we had expected people to have played more than one role.

Our next step explored how often people will play one, two, or even more roles. We thought it unlikely that any one person could play a strong version of every role; similarly, we believed it unlikely that a person would not be able to function effectively in at least one role. Nevertheless, we modeled the percentage of people who assumed no role, one role, two roles, or more than two roles.

TABLE 6. HOW MANY ROLES CAN YOU HAVE?

NUMBER OF ROLES FULFILLED BY INDIVIDUAL EMPLOYEES		
NUMBER OF TEAM ROLES FULFILLED	FREQUENCY	PERCENTAGE (%)
0	9394	6.4
1	45,880	31.5
2	47,615	32.7
3	31,198	21.4
4	11,659	8.0
5	0	0.0
TOTAL	**145,746**	**100.0**

The results confirmed our belief: whereas a few people had played three roles, most had been likely to assume one or two roles, and very few had played four or no roles. No one had played five roles.

The findings also revealed an important lesson. Some people didn't appear to play any role, which would make participating in workshops a disconcerting experience for them. Further analysis showed that these people weren't strong personalities and that they were inclined to fade into the background, fitting into the team without exerting influence. Still, could we say that they would play no role at all? To address this issue, we introduced the concept of role strength to account for the six percent of people who exhibited the no-role profile (see table above). At this point we were able to assess the strength with which one would play a particular psychological role.

We examined how roles would be balanced across different job families. We expected differences to emerge among functionally specialized teams, due to the nature of the people who populate them. Gus and I reasoned, for example, that a managerial team should have fewer people in the Process role than a team of software engineers would. On the other hand, we might be wrong, and we expected most teams to show a rough balance of roles, in any event.

Using the large international sample, we sorted the data into seven broad job families and simulated the distribution of roles:

TABLE 7. ROLES AND JOBS

DISTRIBUTION OF TEAM ROLES BY JOB FAMILY							
ROLE	M&E	PROF	T&S	O&T	S&CS	A&C	S&S
Results	46.2%	41.4%	33.9%	39.2%	53.4%	40.6%	32.1%
Relationships	39.8%	42.4%	36.1%	42.3%	47.2%	39.0%	45.0%
Process	33.1%	43.2%	29.4%	44.1%	38.8%	37.6%	43.4%
Innovation	42.7%	43.8%	36.3%	40.4%	53.5%	39.5%	39.4%
Pragmatism	33.1%	28.7%	36.5%	29.1%	25.8%	32.6%	24.7%
TOTAL	**30,800**	**27,276**	**5,970**	**10,450**	**9,553**	**7,553**	**8,926**

M&E = Managers & Executives; Prof = Professionals; T&S = Technicians & Specialists; O&T = Operations & Trades; S&CS = Sales & Customer Support; A&C = Administrative & Clerical; S&S = Service & Support

The results were fascinating. As seen in the table above, Managers and Executives were likely to have more members who assumed the Results and Innovation roles, which reflected their competitive, ambitious natures. These people would prosper in organizational life, but their mixed roles could cause problems. Sales and Customer Support and Service and Support jobs were more likely to involve Results, Innovation, and Relationship players; these teams were less likely to comprise Pragmatic players. On the other hand, we expected to see more Pragmatists in the Trades and Technicians world, and we did.

Although we worked hard on the report, the real question is whether it can explain what happens at the team level. An earlier discussion involved the case of the finance team who had failed to deliver support for the necessary change to a more commercial, fiscally disciplined organization. The CEO had been grumpy and the team leader bewildered. We profiled the team to see how they showed up:

RESULTS	PRAGMATISM	INNOVATION	PROCESS	RELATIONSHIPS
17	100	0	50	0
People who organize work, clarify roles, coordinate, and provide direction for others. They enjoy taking charge and pushing for results.	People who provide practical, hard-headed evaluations of ideas and proposals. They advocate pragmatic solutions, and their views are not influenced by the need to maintain harmony. They are direct and grounded in reality.	People who recognize when conditions have changed and when the team needs to adapt. They spot emerging trends and patterns quickly, enjoy solving problems, and generate creative solutions.	People who are concerned with implementation, the details of execution, and the use of processes and systems to complete tasks. They are reliable, organized, and conscientious about following procedures.	People who are concerned about morale and how team members are getting along. They are positive and optimistic, attuned to people's feelings, and good at building cohesive relationships.

Figure 21: The Finance Team Revealed

The numbers in the circles above depict the percentage of team members who played that role *strongly*. As the figure shows, the finance team members were the antithesis of natural-born team players. Not one person had been playing the Relationships role; no one had played an Innovation role; few members had assumed the Results role, and virtually *everyone* was hardheaded, practical and skeptical. It was a team of quiet, independent specialists who would neither have shown a great deal of initiative nor have been interested in the messy business of people, relationships, and support.

An excerpt of the report we submitted to the CEO and the finance director read as follows:

> The team profile predicts three key behaviors will get in the way of the team's task:
>
> 1. First, this team will lack drive and prefer getting told what to do. To others, it will come across as reactive and passive.
> 2. Second, the team will avoid building connections. Talkative meetings with line colleagues will be experienced as frustrating or an imposition distracting them from real work. The team will avoid developing relationships with other teams or units.
> 3. Third, this team will lack vision and innovative ability. It is very likely to prefer tried and true methods and will be uncomfortable, uncertain, and unhappy about change. It will react to new ideas by being the black hat, skeptical and excessively concerned with details.

The CEO was grimly delighted with the report. On one hand, it meant that she boldly agreed to change the team, to inject the needed culture shift. New people, with greater drive and a stronger focus on relationships, helped bolster the group. The CEO also replaced the director. On the other hand, the report explained what she intuitively had seen, and the data helped her make informed decisions about staffing. As consultants, we were delighted with the report's diagnostic capability: as intended, it seemed to reveal certain factors concerning the way the team would behave and perform, in addition to how outsiders perceived it.

Understanding an outside perspective is critical. Although hearing what team members say about their team is interesting and can be insightful, teams have a vested interest in explaining away negative behavior. Reports like ours provide a level of rigor and objectivity that forces a team to engage in self-reflection. Insight may not be equal to change, but it's a useful place to start.

THE GENEBANK TEAM

A happier tale can be told about a leadership team who took a hard look at themselves and shifted their behaviors.

When a new CEO took over at GeneBank, a global supplier of dairy and beef genetics, the board gave him a strong mandate to double the size of the business to $1 billion. This was a dramatic shift for a traditional, science-based organization that was deeply suspicious of management. Although its science was superb, the organization had little entrepreneurial skill. Rather, it was sure of its inherent superiority and approached its customers with "we know best" condescension. In the face of growing demand from Asia and of nutraceutical opportunities from the developed world, the board had committed to forgo dividends and to commit a significant capital sum to fund the expansion, which required new skills in business acquisition, global marketing, data science, and logistics. After a business review and reorganization, the CEO recruited a new team.

Our research has shown that the players on top teams are invariably dominant and outgoing, a state of affairs that can hinder the development of psychological safety and of an overarching goal, both of which are essential for team success.

So it proved here; the team over-focused on driving for results and under-focused on process:

Figure 22: The GeneBank Team

Whereas the ESA finance team had a shortage of team members' playing the Results role, the GeneBank team faced the opposite challenge. Their team had an abundance of members' assuming the Results role, a composition that risked fomenting competition:

Figure 23: The GeneBank Team Detail

That functional work groups would attract similar players is unsurprising; for example, research has shown that accountants en masse are unlikely to be perceived as scintillating.[146] But such homogeneity may lead either to intensifying a team's weaknesses or to overplaying its strengths.

GeneBank soon saw the impact of the team's profile. As the board had desired, the team was goal-driven, competitive, and ambitious. The organization, feeling energetic and inspired, increased targets, raised standards, and held individuals accountable. Non-performers quickly exited. The team was exciting to be around; they made a strong effort to connect with each other and with the broader organization.

Nevertheless, the Team Report also revealed a faultline, in the form of a shared derailer.

As discussed above, the GeneBank team members had scored high on Results and were competitive, energetic, and ambitious. They also shared a distinctive, dark-side risk of being Colorful.

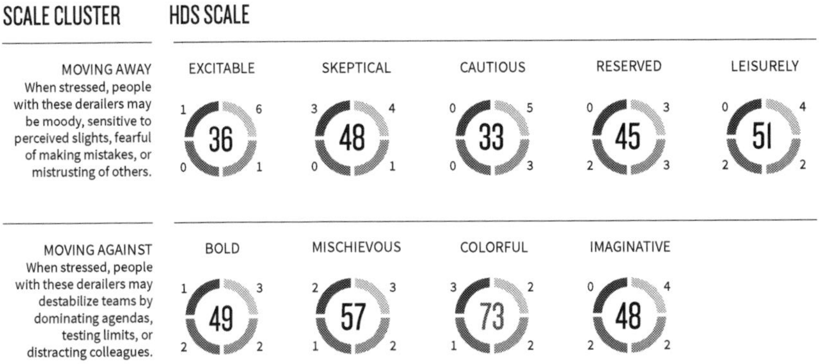

SCALE CLUSTER	HDS SCALE				
MOVING AWAY When stressed, people with these derailers may be moody, sensitive to perceived slights, fearful of making mistakes, or mistrusting of others.	EXCITABLE 1 / 6 / 0 / 1 **36**	SKEPTICAL 3 / 4 / 0 / 1 **48**	CAUTIOUS 0 / 5 / 0 / 3 **33**	RESERVED 0 / 3 / 2 / 3 **45**	LEISURELY 0 / 4 / 2 / 2 **51**
MOVING AGAINST When stressed, people with these derailers may destabilize teams by dominating agendas, testing limits, or distracting colleagues.	BOLD 1 / 3 / 2 / 2 **49**	MISCHIEVOUS 2 / 3 / 1 / 2 **57**	COLORFUL 3 / 2 / 1 / 2 **73**	IMAGINATIVE 0 / 4 / 2 / 2 **48**	

The large number shows the team average score: reading clockwise, the smaller numbers show how many people are low, moderate, moderate-high, and high scorers.

Figure 24: The Dark Side of the GeneBank Team

A meeting of energized, Colorful people can feel like a swirl of vitality. The members can appear to be having a great time, especially as the Colorful behaviors of one person are likely to evoke similar responses from the other Colorful members.

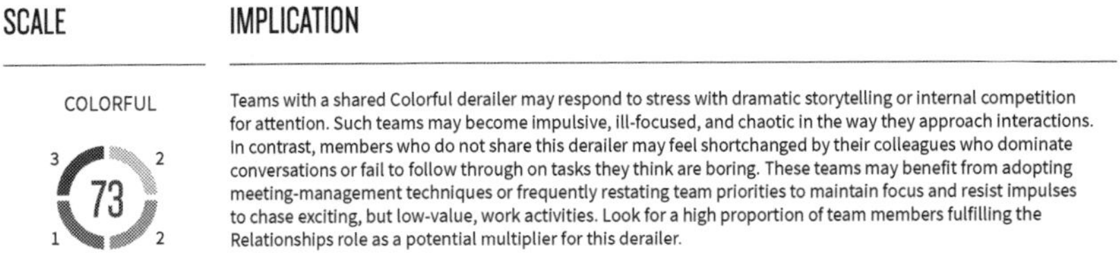

SCALE	IMPLICATION
COLORFUL 3 / 2 / 1 / 2 **73**	Teams with a shared Colorful derailer may respond to stress with dramatic storytelling or internal competition for attention. Such teams may become impulsive, ill-focused, and chaotic in the way they approach interactions. In contrast, members who do not share this derailer may feel shortchanged by their colleagues who dominate conversations or fail to follow through on tasks they think are boring. These teams may benefit from adopting meeting-management techniques or frequently restating team priorities to maintain focus and resist impulses to chase exciting, but low-value, work activities. Look for a high proportion of team members fulfilling the Relationships role as a potential multiplier for this derailer.

Figure 25: The Dark Side Detail

Colorful teams are sociable, easily bored, and move easily from issue to issue. They have trouble staying organized, keeping on top of tasks, and delivering desired outcomes. Observers may notice that the team members are unfocused, distractible, and over-committed.

Because personality derailers are *ego-syntonic*, which is a fancy way of saying that people quite like their derailers, everything seemed to be functioning nicely inside this new and determined team—at least at first. Team members believed that their colorfulness was normal, and they felt comfortable with it. But from the outside, and for the people who reported to the team, the situation became chaotic. Although driven and focused, the team didn't listen to the organization, spending its time in broadcast mode. In addition, goals stacked upon goals as the team emerged from long, strenuous but disorganized meetings. Given the small number of players who assumed a Process role, the team paid no attention to sequencing or resourcing the demands for results.

The GeneBank team had approached their development seriously (after all, they had been tasked with doubling revenue to $1 billion). The CEO was astute; he was aware of the complaints from the organization and publicly committed to change. He commissioned a two-year program of coaching, beginning with thoughtful self-reflection after reading the Team Report. He shared the results of his considerations at a meeting with the direct reports of the executive. He also listened to their grievances about how his team was misbehaving. Then the senior team conducted several memorable round-table sessions with their direct reports. During these sessions, the senior team members were not allowed to offer comments, justifications, explanations, or feedback; instead, they had to listen, paraphrase what they heard, and ask clarifying questions.

The team also engaged in monthly two-hour sessions, during which, using the Team Report profile as a touchstone, they reviewed their collective behavior in meetings, as well as the feedback regarding their public reputation. The team developed behavioral routines and guidelines and published a set of measures against which they would be held accountable.

Finally, each team member, assisted by coaching, developed a plan to address their individual contributions, both negative and positive, to the overall team. The entire team reviewed the resulting plans.

After a few months of the program, the CEO, a strong, experienced, skeptical, analytic leader, confided to me that:

> I got you in as an insurance policy, because frankly, I thought I could simply order them to change. The picture from that report kind of rocked me, though, and I could see that all the new people were so similar we'd just stay locked into our own assumptions about how to behave. It provided us with a way to shift the conversation to be about *us*, and that made the team think of itself as a unit. But don't think you'll get a bonus!

Teams commonly share derailers. When we examined a sample of 675 teams who had taken the HDS, we found that nearly all presented up to three shared derailers. Sometimes a team exhibits no shared derailers, and occasionally they may, incredibly, share as many as nine.

TABLE 8. THE DISTRIBUTION OF DERAILERS

DISTRIBUTION OF SHARED TEAM DERAILERS		
NUMBER	FREQUENCY	PERCENTAGE (%)
0	115	17.0
1	196	29.0
2	126	18.7
3	105	15.6
4	60	8.9
5	35	5.2
6	22	3.3
7	7	1.0
8	7	1.0
9	2	0.3
10	0	0.0
11	0	0.0
TOTAL	**675**	**100.0**

Although individual team members are likely to have their own derailers to manage, shared derailers represent the most likely—and potentially the most problematic—behaviors that may emerge during stressful situations. Of course, there will be occasions where faultlines occur between groups who share derailers, such as a group with Mischievous dark sides and a group with Cautious dark sides; in that event, reconciling the conflicting approaches will be difficult.

VALUES ONE MORE TIME

A final case study illustrates what the HTR can reveal about the effect of shared team values.

This case requires us to enter the specialized world of workplace safety. A 2014 safety report estimated that, globally, approximately 2.5 million deaths (although many suspect that the actual number is considerably higher) occur annually for reasons attributed to work. Even though the biggest component of these deaths is linked to work-related disease, such as cancers from chemical exposure, around 500,000 die from accidents.[147] According to the International Labor Organization, the economic cost of work-related injury and illness varies between two percent and six percent of a nation's gross domestic product.

For example, in 2010, a coal mine explosion on the west coast of New Zealand trapped and incinerated 29 men. Cited as causes of the accident were nonexistent safety equipment, poor training, lax compliance with regulations, and negligence. A general culture of devaluing professional safety practices meant that men ignored and failed to follow safety protocols, conducted merely perfunctory checks, and even shut down essential gas-extraction equipment because it was too noisy.

To mitigate the human and financial cost of workplace accidents and illnesses, most large firms and nearly all governments have instituted departments or agencies that attempt to prevent accidents and promote safety through programs, policies, and interventions. Governments, of course, assume the burden of legislating, inspecting, and enforcing standards, along with the responsibility for prosecuting breaches.

This case concerned the health and safety division (HSD) of a very large mining organization. The mining industry had endured several years of widespread and systemic safety failures, some of which had resulted in worker deaths. Frankly, in the many years of their existence, such failures hadn't much concerned them. But media exposés of some especially egregious safety breaches, plus a *60 Minutes* documentary about the appalling death rate in the coal industry, had led the NZ government to introduce stringent safety legislation that made company directors criminally liable for worker deaths.

Suddenly the coal mining company woke up. They charged a new division, separate from the HR department, with instilling a safety culture and reducing injury rates. However, despite new policies and much stronger powers, six months into the division's mission, the team was meandering and had failed to generate any visible cultural impact.

One of the assumptions that people often make in thinking about team performance is that the most important element is team members' ability to get along.[148] Using that logic, many team-building sessions and interventions focus on soothing issues and reducing conflict. The premise is that once a team is functioning harmoniously, it will have established a firm foundation of trust and can get on with completing its mission.

Unfortunately, that assumption is incorrect.[149] As the Rocket Model emphasizes, what matters more than anything else is that the team has a clear mission and the right people to accomplish it. Without these two elements, a team often becomes a group of people who get together for tea and biscuits. Such socializing was almost the only behavior that the new HSD was performing.

When the HSD completed the Hogan Team Report, the results showed strong similarity in the values they held.

The Team Report assesses values through Hogan's Motives, Values, and Preferences Inventory. This tool measures 10 values:

1. **Recognition:** need for attention, feedback, and praise
2. **Power:** desire for success, status, and control
3. **Hedonism:** desire for a life of diversion, pleasure, and enjoyment
4. **Altruistic:** desire to promote social justice and fairness and to contribute to society
5. **Affiliation:** desire for connection and social interaction
6. **Tradition:** valuing respect, morals, and obligation
7. **Security:** need for predictability, structure, and order

8. **Commerce:** interest in business, business opportunities, and the bottom line
9. **Aesthetics:** need for self-expression and high-quality output
10. **Science:** quest for knowledge, research, technology, and data

We saw with the Chinese Bridge experiment that shared values are useful in helping a team connect and bond, and they influence the approach the team takes towards making judgments and decisions. In the HSD case, the shared values were responsible for a collective bias towards passivity, consensus, and an unworldly approach to work:

POWER

Teams that place little value on Power are often perceived as preferring consensus and disliking competition or disagreement. They usually are more reactive than proactive, value getting along over getting ahead, would rather follow or collaborate than lead, and may have difficulties evaluating others' performance. Others may believe that the team tolerates poor performers or is not sufficiently concerned about achievement, especially if the team has few team members who fulfill the Results role.

COMMERCE

Teams that place little value on Commerce often seem relatively uninterested in financial matters. This team's culture may be one in which relationships and fairness are valued over revenue and profitability, especially if the team also shares Affiliation and Altruistic values. Members of such teams may often undervalue the importance of financial data in managing their business.

The large number shows the team average score: reading clockwise, the smaller numbers show how many people are low, moderate, moderate-high, and high scorers.

Figure 26. Playing it Safe

This collective value set did indeed help the team bond, but in a *negative* direction—that is, they all shared a disinterest (shown by low scores) in things that would help a work team perform effectively. Given that values rarely emerge as a topic of work conversation, the team members had most likely shared a sense that they were fulfilling their roles merely by being together. This team inclined towards being bureaucratic and inward looking, as we discovered when we asked them to complete our assessments. They literally preferred a good cup of tea and a chat to charting new ground.

The Hogan Team Report is a sophisticated tool in that it offers three distinct lenses on the team through understanding roles, derailers, and values. In the case of the health and safety division, a coherent theme emerged from studying all three lenses. Although the team members were likely to bond, they were unlikely to perform. That same story was revealed in every lens we used to understand them.

This bias towards inaction and passivity was dramatically confirmed when we included the team's role composition. We saw that the group comprised a homogenous set of people who were intensely relationship-oriented, but who collectively lacked any drive or ambition. This was a team of kind, warm, genuine people, a team that included neither natural leaders nor hardheaded realists to push them towards achievement.

TEAM SCORE	TEAM ROLE IMPLICATION
RESULTS 0	This team has a low percentage of members who fulfill the Results role, suggesting it is comfortable with collaboration and is unlikely to have difficulties related to internal competition. At their best, such teams are typically willing to work together and share leadership responsibilities. However, at their worst, these teams may also settle for the status quo and seem complacent unless they have clear goals, timelines, and deliverables. The team may need to pay special attention to holding individual members accountable for their commitments. It may also be beneficial to reconfirm targets, set stretch goals, or review the team's performance frequently.
PRAGMATISM 0	This team has a low percentage of members who fulfill the Pragmatism role, suggesting that members may not challenge ideas that, although interesting or innovative, may be highly impractical to implement. At their best, such teams may be willing to stretch the status quo and consider unusual solutions. At their worst, however, such teams may become enamored with abstract solutions that will not work in practice. Such teams often need to find ways to ensure that their plans and solutions are realistic, particularly if the team also has many members who fulfill the Innovation role.
INNOVATION 29	This team has a moderate percentage of members who fulfill the Innovation role, suggesting that it will be able to balance creative vision and long-term strategic perspective with more practical concerns related to implementation of those ideas. At their best, such teams are attuned to changing conditions and how they impact the team's approach to work. At their worst, however, members of these teams may frustrate each other by seeming either negative in the face of good ideas or wildly impractical. Both positions are useful, and the team may need to institute a method to ensure that both views are heard.
PROCESS 29	This team has a low percentage of members who fulfill the Process role, suggesting it will be flexible and adapt quickly to changing business conditions. At their best, such teams may be able to embrace changes and create new approaches as needed. At their worst, however, these teams may lack the self-discipline needed to follow the processes required to execute their plans. Members of such teams may find details boring and planning unnecessary, which may cause the team to seem poorly organized, inefficient, or undisciplined. This may be especially true if the team also has a high percentage of members who fulfill the Innovation role.
RELATIONSHIPS 86	This team has a moderate percentage of members who fulfill the Relationships role, suggesting it includes a mix of gregarious people and tougher-minded colleagues. At their best, such teams can devote adequate attention to internal and external relationships. Members of these teams tend to be united and cohesive, but can still challenge each other and give critical feedback in a constructive manner. At their worst, however, such teams may suffer when more yielding members fail to challenge more blunt colleagues. If communication expectations are considered when matching team members with formal roles, the team should be able to capitalize on this diversity.

Figure 27. The Health and Safety Roles

This configuration of roles is rare. Out of thousands of teams, we've only observed one other team in which no one played two roles. But rare is not the same as impossible, and for this team, the conjunction of people gathered together was profoundly consequential. It was a team that was singularly destined to fail.

Lastly, the nails in their coffin emerged after investigating their shared derailers. The team's shared derailers were Cautious (reluctant to reach decisions under pressure and averse to be caught making a mistake) and Dutiful (the tendency to avoid upsetting the status quo and a desire to conform to authority's rules). In the face of the managers' resistance—which was exactly the situation they were hired to break through—team members tended to acquiesce and fold.

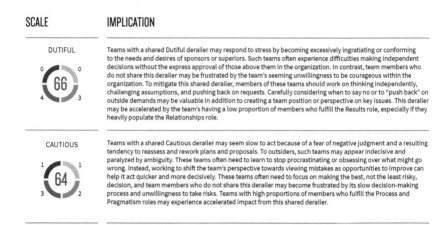

SCALE	IMPLICATION
DUTIFUL 66	Teams with a shared Dutiful derailer may respond to stress by becoming excessively ingratiating or conforming to the needs and desires of sponsors or superiors. Such teams often experience difficulties making independent decisions without the express approval of those above them in the organization. In contrast, team members who do not share this derailer may be frustrated by the team's seeming unwillingness to be courageous within the organization. To mitigate this shared derailer, members of these teams should work on thinking independently, challenging assumptions, and pushing back on requests. Carefully considering when to say no or to "push back" on outside demands may be valuable in addition to creating a team position or perspective on key issues. This derailer may be accelerated by the team's having a low proportion of members who fulfill the Results role, especially if they heavily populate the Relationships role.
CAUTIOUS 64	Teams with a shared Cautious derailer may seem slow to act because of a fear of negative judgment and a resulting tendency to reassess and rework plans and proposals. To outsiders, such teams may appear indecisive and paralyzed by ambiguity. These teams often need to learn to stop procrastinating or obsessing over what might go wrong. Instead, working to shift the team's perspective towards viewing mistakes as opportunities to improve can help it act quicker and more decisively. These teams often need to focus on making the best, not the least risky, decision, and team members who do not share this derailer may become frustrated by its slow decision-making process and unwillingness to take risks. Teams with high proportions of members who fulfill the Process and Pragmatism roles may experience accelerated impact from this shared derailer.

Figure 28: Health and Safety Derailers

Their dark side triggered exactly the wrong behavior, as their conversations focused on risks, the need to get things right, and the imperative to please bosses. The HSD team had a high proportion of individuals who wanted to avoid hard calls or quick decisions out of concern that their decisions would be either wrong or challenged. These circumstances exacerbated the team's tentative, indecisive values and the absence of members who could assume Results and Pragmatist roles.

In this instance, our advice to the CEO was that team coaching was unlikely to change the team, and that he would be better off changing the membership, starting with a stronger, more assertive leader. In light of the recent shift to establish this group, our recommendation signaled a difficult decision for the CEO, one that he was reluctant to make. He persevered for another 12 months, providing stronger and stronger direction for the team. Eventually, he was all but directing their daily activities. But changing deep-seated personality characteristics is a challenging task, all the more so when the group unconsciously reinforces the preferences and habits that need changing.

Two years later, the CEO engineered another restructuring and the team that had gone nowhere went away.

These real-world examples demonstrate the unique worth of examining the group as a whole, rather than looking at it piecemeal, person-by-person. Hogan's Team Report affords a perspective that other tools cannot match. As the GeneBank example shows, teams can collectively learn to reflect on their psychological make-up and institute routines and structured behavioral changes that will enable them to improve.

STRENGTHS ARE NOT THE WHOLE STORY

I had another reason for including examples of problematic teams in this book. Modern human resources departments, management groups, and other organizational entities tend to be vulnerable to fads, such as paying attention to strengths and ignoring weaknesses.

This philosophy plays well in corporate life, but playing only to strengths disregards fatal flaws and faultlines. Working with teams has taught me that people are terrible at recognizing weaknesses because they hold inflated ideas about their own competence. Research by David Dunning of Cornell University has concluded that "the correlation between self-ratings of skill and actual performance in many domains is moderate to meager—indeed, at times, other people's predictions of a person's outcomes prove more accurate than that person's self-predictions."[150]

The GeneBank team, for example, was full of clever, confident and ambitious people who had achieved a great deal—they sat at the top of a large organization with reminders of their success and status all around them. But they began to excel as a team when they considered both their collective weaknesses and their collective strengths and decided to focus on their weaknesses while preserving their strengths.

The Hogan Team Report is a great tool to power team development. It focuses on the team rather than on individuals, it allows for an in-depth view of what the team dynamics will be and why, and it offers teams actionable insights for improvement.

12
THE WINSBOROUGH APPROACH TO TEAM DEVELOPMENT

Remember: upon the conduct of each depends the fate of all.

—— Alexander

Trump University, the fake sales-training organization that the well-known New York real-estate developer (now US president) created, sold its programs through boiler rooms. A boiler room is a high-pressure, outbound-sales call center in which staff typically receive commissions but not salaries. The term "boiler room" refers to places that apply relentless, high-intensity sales tactics on customers and treat staff with an aggressive, demanding and pushy management style.

One of Trump University's main sales outlets was Prosper Inc., headquartered in Provo, Utah. In 2008, as part of the motivational training for a Prosper sales team, the organization held a team-building event. The supervisor, Joshua Christopherson, assembled the team outside and encouraged one member, a man named Chad Hudgens, to lie on his back. Christopherson put a cloth over Hudgens' face and preceded to waterboard him.[151] Waterboarding involves pouring a constant stream of water on the cloth over the victim's mouth; it produces the sensation of drowning and the conviction that death is imminent.

"You saw how hard Chad fought for air right there?" Christopherson asked his team. "Now I want you to go back inside and fight that hard to make sales!" This supervisor also reportedly kept a length of wood on his desk that he called "the 2x4 of motivation."

Yes, this was considered team building. Mind you, so are whitewater rafting, tightrope walking, firewalking, campfire-meeting, cooking, volunteering, and drinking. Hudgens filed suit against his firm, which garnered the name "the waterboarding company." What happened to sales performance after the team-building session doesn't seem to be on record anywhere.

Team building has become popular as a way to jumpstart performance improvements or to resolve poor relationships on the team. Personally, I disapprove of one-off events in which some relentlessly enthusiastic facilitator prods the team into crossing an imaginary, electrified river using 44-gallon drums and short planks, or encourages people into inappropriate self-disclosures that can never be retracted. The image of Ricky Gervais in the original version of *The Office*, encouraging his group to share fantasies during their offsite, remains forever in my head.

TEAM BUILDING

As noted above, effective team performance depends on a number of tightly interconnected mechanisms, one or more of which may not be working well. It makes sense to intervene and fix it. But does team building really work?

Before we answer that question, distinguishing between team building and team development is useful.

Team building is typically aimed at promoting both task and group cohesion. Done well, it particularly targets the early stages of the Rocket Model to ensure that team members are clear about their mission and that they become acquainted with one another:[152]

TABLE 9. TEAM BUILDING

TEAM BUILDING	MAIN OBJECTIVES
Designed to improve interpersonal relations and social interactions and to clarify tasks and roles. Used to address problems occurring in teams.	1. Setting goals 2. Developing trust and resolving conflict 3. Clarifying roles 4. Solving problems and making decisions

With this focus, team building is worthy and laudable. On the other hand, as the waterboarding example illustrated, team building is more appropriately described as an industry of activities in search of a need. Practitioners too frequently lack any understanding of the psychology of teams. That's why activities like indoor go-karting, karaoke, whitewater rafting, and treetop rope courses often advertise themselves as team-building activities.

Two other reasons explain how the activity industry and bad practitioners continue to make a living. The people who become team leaders are often subject- matter experts who have been promoted into leading teams, despite their lack of training and skill. The second reason is that corporate HR departments tend to seek quick fixes and are likely to be unaware of the scientific principles that underlie team development.

Here is the critical point: The team-building exercise is not an end in itself.

For the most part, trust falls aren't part of anyone's daily activity, and are unlikely to change the team dynamic. Unless they go wrong!

Figure 29. Trust Fall Failure

Participating in team activities can be fun. Wine tasting is fun, darts down at the pub are fun, and paintballing is fun. Establishing social connections is healthy. However, activities are not the same as team building. Actually, as the following story demonstrates, paintballing as a team-building event might best be left to the military.

Several years ago, things didn't go well for Peter Brooks when his former employer bused his work group to a suburban Washington, D.C. field. They were divided into teams for a round of paintball: "We were issued safety goggles and paintball guns, one of which immediately misfired. It hit a district manager in the crotch," Brooks recalled.

He remembers that the game quickly devolved into screaming, pleading, and retaliatory rage—the paintballs left large welts: "A lot of people pointed their guns right at their supervisors, me included," Brooks said. "I shot mine right in the middle of the back, and then when he spun around with revenge in his eyes, I surrendered."

"The bus ride home," Brooks recalled, "was dead silent."[153]

True team building *doesn't* target skill-based competencies. Rather, its purpose is to help individuals and groups examine, diagnose, and act to change their behavior and improve their interpersonal relationships.[154] Team building typically takes place in informal settings away from work and is most often a one-day event. Teams progress through a set of activities that encourages information sharing and fosters the team's shared commitment to a goal. Done well, team building should have clear aims and objectives, and the exercises should relate directly to both the goal *and* the work of the team.

Such interventions have considerable face validity (which means they look as if they should exert an impact on the team), and consultants develop the day's program from lessons that practice has taught them.

But is it effective?

Eduardo Salas in Florida has conducted the most comprehensive research on this question.[155] By examining the combined results of numerous studies, he and his colleagues reached the conclusion that well-designed and well-delivered team building improves team outcomes—somewhat. From a scientific perspective, the relations are best described as encouraging rather than definitive. Of particular interest is that Salas pinpointed that, out of all the activities that team building entails, the goal-setting and role-clarification components had the largest effect on team outcomes. This result fits with having found that hard factors exercise a more immediate and direct effect on team performance than do soft factors.

These discoveries matter because, as Harvard's Amy Edmondson points out, stable, clearly defined teams are less and less in evidence, although teaming, as a skill, is on the rise.[156] Team-building methodologies that facilitate useful interactions to improve processes and to facilitate interpersonal relationships are becoming necessary.

In summary, team leaders, by all means, should undertake team building. To be clear, though, they should not expect a radical uptick in team performance. Be aware, as well, that for many people, offsite adventures and trust falls were gladly left behind at school.

TEAM DEVELOPMENT

Team development, on the other hand, focuses on improving the collective capabilities, routines, and skills of teams on the job. As suspicious as I am about one-off team building, I am deeply committed to the idea of team coaching and development.

The key elements of the development approach are summarized below:

TABLE 10. TEAM DEVELOPMENT

TEAM DEVELOPMENT	MAIN OBJECTIVES
Instructional methods to train and coach the whole team's performance on key skills and competencies (as in the hard, soft & deep) To prepare teams prior to performing, to coach them in action, and to address team breakdowns	1. Focus on the team first and individuals second. 2. Promote team-focused knowledge, skills, and attitudes (KSAs) for effective performance. 3. Practice these KSAs in a safe environment and enable skill-transfer to the work environment. 4. Provide structured feedback to teams and individuals.

The science supporting these types of carefully structured interventions is strong, and reviews of team-performance interventions report more powerful impacts for team development and training than they do for team building.[157] The military, NASA, and elite sports franchises all subscribe to the team-development approach. In fact, if more organizations and leaders were as committed to treating their teams in as professional a manner as those organizations, the US could expect a significant increase in productivity.

Crew resource management training (CRT), which we previously described, is a sound example of team-based proficiency development. Through CRT, individuals learn to operate efficiently with others, thereby promoting shared awareness and preventing the selfish, macho individualism that doomed United Airlines flight 173. One key CRT skill, for example, is shared situational awareness—remaining mindful and attentive to important environmental information. Although that dictum might sound like common sense, achieving it as a team skill requires verifying that one's colleagues are equally aware of the environment and are not diverted or distracted. On the sports field, situational awareness signifies tracking the opposition, the ball, the location of one's own players, and the players' physical and mental state—all the while integrating the current play and considering options. In billiards, the necessary strategizing transpires in a player's head, but in sports teams, situational awareness is a noisy skill; players continuously call to each other, bellow warnings across the field, touch each other, and check in with teammates. It is also a skill that relies on a climate of psychological safety (so that teammates respect one another's calls) and commitment to the team goal (so individuals don't try to reap individual glory).

Whereas team building endeavors to establish the precursors of teamwork, team development focuses on teamworking skills and on creating a group-based identity. Development necessarily focuses on the team as the unit to develop. I stress this point because, first, careful team development is rarely done in work settings, and, second, coaches and leaders frequently fail to grasp the value of understanding the group as a whole.

To underscore this point, consider a shift that is occurring in hiring practices. The hyper-competitive environment of Silicon Valley is beginning to appreciate the value that accrues in stable, well-developed teams. Investors regularly assess the effectiveness of a company's executive team when they're deciding which businesses to fund. Why not do the same for functional teams down the hierarchy?

A payments company called Stripe evaluated teams in a unique way. They were frustrated with hiring single developers and began an initiative called "Bring Your Own Team." They offered to interview small teams of engineers and hire them en masse and immediately if they successfully passed the screening process. Stripe's belief was that employees are more productive when they're part of a team that they've worked with before. It's too early to see if the approach has worked, but it's a fascinating experiment.

Figure 30. Hiring as Part of a Team Is Already Here

Another startup, Elevator, is trying to create a marketplace based on hiring entire teams. "There's a lot of power in teams," Elevator Cofounder and CEO Mike Anderson said. "Who does the team really belong to? They know as a group they can build and ship products on day one. If you're ready to go, why should you have to leave your team?"[158] If Elevator finds a match for the team in a new company, the whole team quits their jobs at once, moves to the new location, and keeps working together.

Although the individual-centric tendencies of typical management may be showing signs of fraying, other forces mean these changes will take a while to emerge. Tomas Chamorro-Premuzic argues that narcissism, a personality trait characterized by unrealistically positive self-views, overconfidence, and entitlement, has been on the rise for some time and is higher in millennials than in other generations.[159] Chamorro-Premuzic suggests that narcissism will exert a negative impact on teams because narcissistic individuals seek to fulfill their own needs before considering the team. More than ever, teaming will become a conscious act that requires support, commitment, and training, especially for leaders.

The answer to Chamorro-Premuzic's concern lies in the challenge that everyone faces—how to manage the tension between wanting to advance one's own interests and the desire to get along with others. This tension may explain why smaller teams tend to work better: because the number of relationships that need to be managed increases exponentially with team size; balancing getting ahead with getting along becomes more difficult as more relationships enter the mix. For humans, leadership evolved in an effort to solve that problem, which means that one of a leader's key tasks is to suppress team members' individualistic tendencies and to channel their energies into meeting the group's needs.

But do leaders invest their time in managing teams? In 2004, Richard Hackman asked team leaders and members to rank the amount of attention the team leader gave to each of four activities:

1. Structuring the team and its tasks
2. Coaching individuals
3. Running external interference
4. Coaching the whole team

In both the leader and the member reports, coaching the team as a whole came in last. So, to play this tune one more time: Coaching the whole team really matters.

HOW TO WORK WITH THE HARD, THE SOFT AND THE DEEP

In working with the hard, the soft, and the deep aspects of teaming, my consulting firm, Winsborough Limited, developed a team-coaching methodology to take advantage of tools like the Hogan Team Report (HTR). This approach emerged from reading the research findings on team effectiveness, our work in developing the Hogan Team Report, and many years of coaching real teams that were trying to improve their performance and overcome obstacles.

What we do is not particularly innovative or special. The Winsborough approach is structured and research based, which sets it apart from most team interventions. We refuse to conduct single, one-day team-building events, asking teams instead to commit to a one-year coaching program. We've done this work for hundreds of senior leadership teams, project teams, and functional groups, as well as for elite sports and combat teams. We've also applied the methodology to two multi-year, large-scale road construction projects.

The process we follow is straightforward and deals sequentially with the hard, soft, and deep aspects of high-performance teamwork. While it sounds simple, in practice it's as messy as the real-world demands. Still, not having a plan is like leaping from a tall building and trying to crochet a parachute on the way down.

Below, I have provided just a few examples of the interventions and approaches we take. Feel free to appropriate them for yourself.

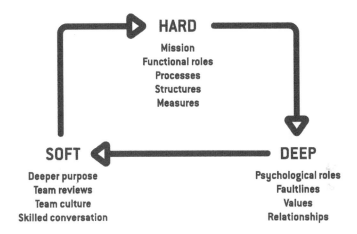

Figure 31. The Hard, Soft & Deep of Team Developmnet

When a team forms, the first order of business should always be to ensure that everyone understands what they are there to achieve. If that statement sounds too obvious, one might consider that, among the dozen senior leadership teams Winsborough surveyed in 2007, only one team expressed unanimous agreement when asked about their mission.

Our initial meetings and off-sites are tailored to clarify:

- Who is on the team and who is not
- The short-, medium-, and long-term priorities
- Each person's responsibilities
- How success will be measured
- How the team will work together and run its processes
- How it will meet, make decisions, and review its performance
- The assets and liabilities
- The context for performance

The Rocket Model is an ideal tool to use at this time, either as a framework or as a questionnaire, because it guides teams through the key hard elements of goal setting, measurement, task skills, and functional team roles, which, taken together, form the basis of high performance. No one can develop a team in the absence of a mission or purpose, and to unlock its performance, the team must understand and accept its mission.

For example, functional roles are best defined early, clarified with the whole team, and refined over time in response to emerging task contingencies. Implementing this strategy avoids role stress, a well-recognized source of team dissatisfaction and a prime reason for exits. Nevertheless, role stress is a predictable and logical consequence of failing to regularly review and adjust individual tasks.[160] In early sessions with any team, we establish and review role understanding at the individual and team level, partly for clarity, but also to ensure that the team is skilled at discussing role descriptions.

One of the tools Winsborough developed to help teams discuss roles is to ask team members to swap roles. Then their task is to articulate what other people do. We review the results of the questionnaire with the team leader, highlighting the importance of clarifying the mission and ensuring that all members understand their functional roles. We also share the results with the whole team at an offsite, reinforcing that team members understand and endorse the mission and agree with any team-development plans.

To help teams maintain a professional focus, we encourage them to communicate clearly and *formally* what their mission is and what will constitute success. For example, on the road construction project I discussed previously, we developed huge signboards showing realistic images of the finished structure that embodied the team's mission. These boards were popular with the work crews and inspired enthusiastic ownership and collective pride, especially during open days and dignitary visits. Knowledge-based teams can replicate this tactic by developing and posting strong statements about their upcoming accomplishments or by creating personas that represent their end users.

Management and leadership teams may want to formalize other hard aspects of high-performance teamwork. We often collaborate with top-leadership teams to draft a team charter—not of vague and clichéd precepts, but of roles, hard performance measures, and behavioral guidelines. These charters also establish who has decision rights.

The best teams expend substantial effort in clarifying their understanding of the mission, team roles, and team performance. This strategy is particularly noticeable for senior leadership teams, in which distinguishing the boundaries between one's functional role and one's team-leadership role can be difficult. As an example, the following figure shows part of the charter from the top-leadership team of an Australian federal agency, confirming what they would and would not do:

WHAT WE DO

1. Have a good time at work.
2. Articulate context, direction and the path for the organisation.
3. Set principles, not rules.
4. Build good relationships; recruit sister agencies to help; connect with the wider Public Service.
5. Governance: fit the organization to our strategy; Monitor their success and performance.
6. Grow good leaders.
7. Tolerate risk & mistakes as part of developing the organisation.

WHAT WE DON'T

1. Do the work of policy development.
2. Deal with lots of paper – short is good.
3. Act as a court for arguments – resolve them lower down.
4. Re-hash decisions we've made.
5. Manage individual budgets.
6. Tell managers how to allocate resources.
7. Rain on other people's excitement, ever.

Figure 32. Team Charter

A charter like this can formalize the insights that the Rocket Model provides and ensure that everyone is aware of what's expected. Moreover, they provide the team practice in developing the skill of thinking together—forming a mental model or shared understanding. Mental models require developing shared situational awareness. They also involve collective intelligence and transactive memory, the knowledge that team members distribute among themselves. For example, what would happen if our hypothetical crew flying to Mars had an unfortunate encounter with a meteorite while the crew medic was alone on watch? In the best possible scenario, the medic would have been cross-trained to initiate emergency procedures and would assemble the relevant crew members to deal with the hull damage and the loss of air pressure.

EXPLORING THE DEEP DRIVERS OF PERFORMANCE

Once teams have spent time building a basis for high-performing teamwork, we ease them, after about three months, into examining the deep elements of their team. We use the HTR to guide this process, working through roles, values, and finally, faultlines.

The reason we wait before exploring team dynamics is to allow the sense of urgency that accompanies the early stages of team formation to dissipate. Teams take time to settle, to develop a shared appreciation for their task and to let a social hierarchy emerge. This settling process is almost entirely unconscious, as team members evaluate one another's strengths, weaknesses, and personalities, and begin to build working relationships.

We also want the team to get the hard aspects right and to spend time implementing them. Team development done too quickly just dumps data on the team and leaves them with a long list of well-intentioned actions.

Because the HTR offers such a rich depth of information, we use it as an input for team discussions and explorations over months.

We begin by individually debriefing the team members, exploring their perception of their functional role before discussing how their psychological roles could exert the most effective impact on the team's mission. We prefer to address these topics outside a team session, so that individuals will not be surprised by information that may surface later. Creating psychological safety is crucial; facilitators must work to shape it and do nothing to undermine it.

We also engage the team leader in two or three sessions to review the HTR. We maintain the conversation at the level of the team as a whole and work to develop the leader's understanding of the team's strengths, as well as its developmental needs.

As leaders explore the HTR, they often express a desire to cut certain team members, or they recommend that they need to build out this or that role by adding someone else to the team. Resist the temptation to follow either course of action. Instead, team leaders should play the hand they have been dealt: they should develop the current team into a high-performing unit and help team members perform at their maximum potential. Cleaving to a shallow, quick opinion about an individual's fit or competence sends a bad message to the rest of the crew.

The most favorable outcome of the team leader sessions is to have generated a set of observations and questions about the relationships among team roles, derailers, values, and team performance. Generating hypotheses—not answers—is the critical step at this point.

AVOIDING SHEEP DIPS

New Zealand is frequently associated with sheep—and sheep jokes. Yes, the country raised multitudes of sheep and exported the best lamb in the world. In fact, once upon a time, sheep outnumbered New Zealanders by hundreds to one. As a result, sheep metaphors abound—and one of the best refers to how sheep were once put through a mini-swimming pool filled with a solution that prevented parasites, called a sheep dip. The term eventually came to represent an approach to personnel training—a one-off, quick plunge into a topic, after which the person could be considered trained.

When it comes to team development, don't use a sheep dip.

Our initial deep dive sessions explore the team's functional and psychological roles. The fundamental element underlying our work is discoveries—a term provided by my Danish colleague, Joan Jakobsen. In working with teams, Jakobsen asks the members to share their observations of how roles (and values and derailers) manifest themselves at work. Team members use post-it notes to record their reflections about specific examples of the team's best and worst functioning and the specific lessons they can draw from these reflections, regarding how the team's role composition affects its work.

This approach is useful, insofar as it pushes the team to contemplate its own behavior and performance and generates an awareness of the reputation the team is likely to establish. Again, we stress to teams the value of thinking about themselves as a unit before focusing their analysis on individuals. After they have created a suitable overview, they can develop plans and strategies to mitigate role gaps, deal with blind spots, and remedy faultlines.

Over the next three months the Team Report will form the backdrop to conversations and planning meetings. We work to keep the team aware of the report's insights and coach members in linking their successes and failures to their behavior.

BUILDING COHESION AND CONSCIOUSLY STRIVING FOR HIGH PERFORMANCE

Team trust is not a given at the beginning. It grows from repeated, predictable, and benevolent interactions, reinforced by sound team institutions (e.g., fair treatment, open communication, transparent measures, and feedback), good leadership, and an absence of shirkers.

Unlike most team-building interventions, Winsborough doesn't explore individual team member's contributions until the team has established a sound basis of trust and a climate of psychological safety. As I have stressed throughout this book, these elements aren't magic; only a basic understanding of how teams operate can facilitate their development.

Two interventions that we use to produce high-performance teamwork are deepening interpersonal knowledge and trust and after-action reviews. Jon Katzenbach, a past McKinsey partner and author, has remarked that members of top-performing teams develop a deep, emotional, and shared commitment to each other's success, independent of the team's mission. Among the dozens of teams I have coached, I think I have observed this phenomenon only a handful of times—but the experience is transcendent and profoundly moving. This level of commitment can propel a team to extraordinary performance.

For example, the top leadership team of a government agency with whom I worked for five years certainly demonstrated it. On one memorable occasion, team members shared their concerns with a colleague about his performance, prompting deeply personal, searing conversations about how they might help and generating a set of options for action—including leaving the organization. Ultimately, the team member chose the option to leave, with neither rancor nor recrimination, but instead, with a strong measure of support and even love.

To develop this measure of trust and regard for colleagues takes time, but structured, guided activity can accelerate it. Winsborough prompts the process by facilitating deep dives among team members, using the HTR as a springboard. Deep dives involve three sessions:

1. **Values**

   During the values session, we ask team members to share their motivations and interests, both within and outside of work. They explore common values and search for examples of how their values have aligned with their decisions or their assumptions about what is important. We use the concept of implicit bias (pervasive preconceptions that operate under the radar of human consciousness and influence how we see and treat others) to explore shared blind spots.[161] Finally, we engage the whole team in discussing shared values' role in creating a team culture and the implications of that culture, in terms of fitting into the wider organizational culture, and managing their own mission.

2. **Roles**

   We conduct a guided conversation between the team members about roles a little like a speed-dating session. The encounters start out at 10 minutes per person and drop by one minute during subsequent sessions (because we find that information tends to become repetitive towards the end). The object is for each person to develop insights about the psychological role(s) they play most and least on the team. Team members start the conversation by asking a short set of questions:

   a. What psychological roles do you know I play?
   b. How do I show up in them? What have you seen from me?
   c. How does that affect the morale and life of our team? What about the impact I have on our performance?

    d. What could I do more of? Less of?

    e. What do you think we need to collectively pay more attention to?

The rules of the speed dates are that players cannot make excuses, explain, or justify any of the comments, but they can ask questions to clarify. The session ends with members sharing what they learned and what they commit to doing differently to enhance the team's performance.

3. **Derailers**

The final deep dive explores the dark side of the team's individual behavior on the team. Obviously, addressing this topic requires the team to have established a solid foundation of trust, which is identifiable by a high comfort level with self-disclosure and the ability to provide strong feedback. If these conditions don't exist, or if the team is under significant pressure, don't do this exercise.

We begin by revisiting the collective dark side of the team, and having the team summarize how those derailers impact their performance or their reputation. Those team members who do not share the derailer can give their impression of how it affects the team, while those who do share the derailer must listen in silence. The member receiving the feedback then summarizes the feedback, and we record the impacts on a flip chart.

Because derailers are frequently unconscious and typically constitute coping mechanisms, identifying the behaviors they drive can be difficult. It isn't uncommon for people to enjoy the effect that the derailer produces, or they enjoy the feeling that comes when they deploy it in social settings. Therefore, after dissecting each shared derailer, the team spends time developing both individual and team responses, including identifying situational triggers and reinforcers (such as a leadership team who might take perverse delight in terrifying staff who present to them). The team then develops mitigation strategies, and then we begin work on individual plans.

CONSCIOUS PERFORMANCE REVIEW

The second approach we devote to developing cohesion involves conscious, reflective reviews of the team's performance (what they have achieved) and processes (how they have achieved it). The US Army, for whom learning and improving is literally a matter of life or death, built the model of *before-action reviews* and *after-action reviews*. After-action reviews (AARs) originated in the early 1990s at the US Army National Training Center in California. They were used to integrate lessons from large-scale war games more successfully and to construct more effective learning capabilities at the organization level:

> Imagine an organization that confronts constantly changing competitors. That is always smaller and less well-equipped than its opponents. That routinely cuts its manpower and resources. That turns over a third of its leaders every year. And that still manages to win competition after competition after competition.

> The U.S. Army's Opposing Force (commonly known as OPFOR), a 2,500-member brigade whose job is to help prepare soldiers for combat, is just such an organization ... OPFOR engages units-in-training in a variety of mock campaigns under a wide range of conditions. Every month, a fresh brigade of more than 4,000 soldiers takes on OPFOR, which, depending on the scenario, may play the role of a hostile army or insurgents, paramilitary units, or terrorists. The two sides battle on foot, in tanks, and in helicopters dodging artillery, land mines, and chemical weapons. Stationed on a vast, isolated stretch of California desert, OPFOR has the home-court advantage. But the force that's being trained—called Blue Force, or BLUFOR, for the duration of the exercise—is numerically and technologically superior. It possesses more dedicated resources and better, more rapidly available data. It is made up of experienced soldiers. And it knows just what to expect, because OPFOR shares its methods from previous campaigns with BLUFOR's commanders. In short, each of these very capable BLUFOR brigades is given practically every edge. Yet OPFOR almost always wins.

Underlying OPFOR's consistent success is the way it uses the *after-action review* (AAR), a method for extracting lessons from one event or project and applying them to others.[162]

We have modified the army's after-action steps, but the process remains deceptively simple:

1. What was our goal or intent?
2. What were the actual outcomes?
3. What caused the results we got?
4. What went well and should be sustained?
5. What surprised us?
6. What needs improvement?
7. What are the changes we need to make?

Our experience and evidence suggests that, for the most part, AARs fail because they devolve into a checkbox exercise. Another way to think of the difference between getting the value this tool offers and simply going through the motions is to imagine a string quartet, whose players are all new to each other, playing a composition for the first time. The result is likely to be subpar. Instead, the players must play a movement, stop and critique their own performance, design improvements, make adjustments, give each other feedback, and repeat the process.

It works the same for effective teams. Rather than considering the activity to be a checkbox exercise, successful teams treat the process professionally. They work through the list, starting with defining the goal and then exploring what

happened. But too many of the teams with whom we have worked have presented false accounts, either to save face or because their derailers prevented them from accepting a less-than-pleasant truth about their performance. In contrast, the members of effective teams check their egos and encourage their teammates to critique their actions and provide feedback. The discipline of after-action reviews is daunting to maintain, and more daunting still to execute.

ENDPIECE

Teams are consequential in the lives of most people, one way or another. Perhaps more than that, we've seen that teams are fundamental to nearly all human affairs. Because our most basic psychology emerges from the fact that we are all group-dwelling animals, teamwork and cooperation developed as a super-cooperation technology that enabled us to adapt and thrive in every available ecological niche, including the extreme cold of the Arctic, the highest mountains of Nepal or Peru, the baking hot deserts of the Kalahari, and the fertile, easy plains and prairies of America, Asia, and Europe. At this point, our mastery of the planet is nearly complete. The only animals whose effectiveness at surviving comes close to rivaling ours are other super-cooperators like ants.

> High performance results only from aligning the hard, soft, and deep aspects of teamwork.

So deeply woven into our shared psyche is the fundamental technology of teamwork that at times we barely notice it, or we take it for granted—as if we take for granted that people will drop everything to help strangers who are facing devastation and disaster. In taking such altruism for granted, we assume that teamwork will simply be there when needed—or when ordered by a leader who fails to understand human nature and human behavior.

High performance results only from aligning the hard, soft, and deep aspects of teamwork. The hard aspects tell us that every team needs a point, a purpose, or a mission. Everyone on the team must understand and share the mission before anyone can coordinate the team's activities. In addition, team members must be proficient in delivering the necessary skills.

The soft aspects of teamwork tell us that our *social* architecture is equally important to fostering effective teamwork. Ensuring fairness and equity is essential to developing trust among team members and trust between the team and its leader.

Coordinating effectively with one another requires constant communication and the ability to overcome roadblocks and conflicts. If these skills are underdeveloped, the most competent group of people in the world will flounder and fail.

Finally, we saw that the deep aspects of personality exert a substantial impact on teamwork. Team composition, including the team's thinking and behavior styles, its response to stress, and its values, combine to drive team dynamics.

For me, the good news is that the technology for producing more successful teams, teams that also provide enjoyment and rewards for their members, is available and open-source. If you are on your own journey working with teams, as a leader or as a coach or team member, then heed the words of the coach of the San Antonio Spurs, Gregg Popovich: "It's not about any one person. You've got to get over yourself and realize that it takes a group to get this thing done."

Which, of course, is the point. Effective, successful, high-performing teams are living, active entities in their own right. They are born of a shared need and sustained through team members' continuous focus on achieving the goal, on sustaining a shared understanding, and on turning individual behaviors towards the greater good.

And when the need goes away, so should the team—until the next time.

REFERENCES

1. Tomasello, M. (2014). The ultra-social animal. *European Journal of Social Psychology*, *44*(3), 187–194.

2. Wilson, E. O. (2012). *The social conquest of Earth*. New York, NY: Liveright Pub. Corp.

3. Henrich, J. (2016). *The secret of our success: How culture is driving human evolution, domesticating our species, and making us smarter*. Princeton, NJ: Princeton University Press.

4. Warneken, F., Chen, F., & Tomasello, M. (2006). Cooperative activities in young children and chimpanzees. *Child Development*, *77*(3), 640–663.

5. Becchio, C., Adenzato, M., & Bara, B. G. (2006). How the brain understands intention: Different neural circuits identify the componential features of motor and prior intentions. *Consciousness and Cognition*, *15*(1), 64–74.

6. Hennessy, J. J. (2015). *The first battle of Manassas: An end to innocence, July 18–21, 1861*. Mechanicsburg, PA: Stackpole Books.

7. Haidt, J., Seder, J. P., & Kesebir, S. (2008). Hive psychology, happiness and public policy, *Journal of Legal Studies*, *37*, 133–156.

8. Sherif, M., Harvey, O. J., White, B. J., Hood, W., & Sherif, C. (1961/1954). *Intergroup conflict and cooperation: The Robbers Cave experiment*. Norman, OK: University of Oklahoma Institute of Group Relations.

9. Haidt, J., Seder, J. P., & Kesebir, S. (2008). Hive psychology, happiness and public policy, *Journal of Legal Studies*, *37*, 133–156

10. Tajfel, H. (1974). Social identity and intergroup behavior. *Social Science Information*, *13*(2), 65–93.

11. Fehr, E., Fischbacher, U., & Gächter, S. (2002). Strong reciprocity, human cooperation, and the enforcement of social norms. *Human Nature*, *13*(1), 1–25.

12. Haidt, J. (2012, September 4). *The righteous mind: Why good people are divided by politics and religion*. New York, NY: Pantheon.

13. The Edge. (2012). Conversation with Joseph Henrich. Retrieved from https://www.edge.org/conversation/joseph_henrich-how-culture-drove-human-evolution

14. Winsborough, D., Kaiser, R. B., & Hogan, R. (2009). An evolutionary view: What followers want from their leaders. *Leadership in Action*, *29*(3), 8–11.

15. Adair, J. (1973). *Action-centered leadership*. New York: McGraw-Hill.

16. Hogan, Robert. (2007). *Personality and the fate of organizations*. Mahway, NJ: Lawrence Erlbaum Associates Publishers.

17. MacMullen, R. (1984). *Christianizing the Roman Empire: AD 100–400*. New Haven, CT: Yale University Press.

18. Buettner, R., & Bagli, C. V. (2016, June 11). How Donald Trump bankrupted his Atlantic City casinos but still earned millions. Retrieved from http://www.nytimes.com/2016/06/12/nyregion/donald-trump-atlantic-city.html?_r=0

19. Rozovsky, J. (2015, November 17). The five keys to a successful Google team. Retrieved from https://rework.withgoogle.com/blog/five-keys-to-a-successful-google-team/

20. Peterson, M., Wilson, J. F.: The culture-work-health model and work stress. *American Journal of. Health Behavior, 2002, 26*,16–24.

21. Stewart, M. (2009). *The management myth: Why the experts keep getting it wrong*. New York, NY: W. W. Norton and Company.

22. Deloitte. (2016). *Global human capital trends 2016*. Retrieved from http://www2. deloitte.com/content/dam/Deloitte/global/Documents/HumanCapital/gx-dup-global-human-capital-trends-2016.pdf

23. Cummings, T. G. and Worley, C. G. (2009). *Organization development and change*. Mason, Ohio: Cengage Learning.

24. O'Toole, J., and Lawler, E. E. (2006). *The new American workplace*. New York: Palgrave Macmillan.

25. Robbins, H. & Finley, M. (2000). *The new why teams don't work*. San Francisco, CA: Berrett-Koehler.

26. McChrystal, S., Silverman, D., Fussell, C. & Collins, T. (2015, June 9). General Stanley McChrystal:How the military can teach us to adapt. Retrieved from http://time.com/3904177/mcchrystal-team-of-teams/

27. Torrente, P., Salanova, M., Llores, S. & Schaufeli, W. (2012). Teams make it work: How team work engagement mediates between social resources and performance in teams *Psicothema, 24,* 106-112

28. Winsborough, D., & Marshall, B. (2007). Winsborough senior team benchmark report. Retrieved May 26, 2016 from http://bit.ly/1XVfELv

29. Bradley, B. H., Klotz, A. C., Postlethwaite, B. E., & Brown, K. G. (2012). Ready to rumble: How team personality composition and task conflict interact to improve performance. *Journal of Applied Psychology, 98(2),* 385–392.

30. Gawande, A. (2002). *Complications: A surgeon's notes on an imperfect science*. New York, Metropolitan Books. Gawande, A. (2010). *The checklist manifesto: How to get things right*. New York: Metropolitan Books.

31. MacCoun, R. J. & Hix, W. M. (2010). Unit cohesion and military performance. In *Sexual Orientation and U.S. Military Personnel Policy: An Update of RAND's 1993 Study*. Santa Monica: RAND.

32. Tesluk, P., Mathieu, J. E., Zaccaro, S. J., & Marks, M. (1997). Task and aggregation issues in the analysis and assessment of team performance. *Team Performance Assessment and Measurement: Theory, Methods, and Applications,* 197–224.

33. Coutu, Diane, and M. Beschloss. (2009). Why teams don't work. *Harvard Business Review, 87*(5), 98–105.

34. Bennett, D. (2013). The Dunbar number, from the guru of social networks. *Bloomberg BusinessWeek*.

35. Knapton, S. (2016, January 12). Facebook users have 155 friends—but would trust just four in a crisis. Retrieved from http://www.telegraph.co.uk/news/science/science-news/12108412/Facebook-users-have-155-friends-but-would-trust-just-four-in-a-crisis.html

36. Dunbar, R. I. M. (2013, November 4). Robin Dunbar on Dunbar numbers. Retrieved from http://www.socialsciencespace.com/2013/11/robin-dunbar-on-dunbar-numbers/

37. Staats, B. R., Milkman, K. L., & Fox, C. R. (2012). The team scaling fallacy: Underestimating the declining efficiency of larger teams. *Organizational Behavior and Human Decision Processes, 118(2)*, 132–142.

38. Edmonson, A. (2012). *Teaming: How organizations learn, innovate, and compete in the knowledge economy*. San Francisco, CA: Wiley.

39. Takeuchi, H., & Nonaka, I. (1986). The new new product development game. *Harvard Business Review, 64(1)*, 137–146.

40. Walther, S. (2012, August 17). Scrum in 5 minutes. Retrieved from http://stephenwalther.com/archive/2012/08/17/scrum-in-5-minutes

41. King, R. (1998). Jeans therapy: Levi's factory workers are assigned to teams, and morale takes a hit. *Wall Street Journal, 3232*, A1, A6.

42. Shuffler, M. L., Diaz-Granados, D., & Salas, E. (2011). There's a science for that: Team development interventions in organizations. *Current Directions in Psychological Science, 20(6)*, 365–372.

43. Wiseman, F. & Sangit C. (2003). Team payroll and team performance in major league baseball: 1985–2002. *Economics Bulletin, 1*, 1–10.

44. Breunig, R., Garrett-Rumba, B., Jardin, M., & Rocaboy, Y. (2014). Wage dispersion and team performance: A theoretical model and evidence from baseball. *Applied Economics, 46(3)*, 271–281.

45. Swaab, R. I., Schaerer, M., Anicich, E. M., Ronay, R., & Galinsky, A. D. (2014). The too-much-talent effect: Team interdependence determines when more talent is too much or not enough. *Psychological Science, 25(8)*, 1581–1591.

46. Leeson, P. (2009). *The invisible hook: The hidden economics of pirates*. Princeton, NJ: Princeton University Press.

47. Leeson P. (2009) The invisible hook: The law and economics of pirate tolerance. *New York Univ. J. Law Library, 4*:139–171

48. Casciaro, T. & Sousa Lobo, M. (2008). When competence is irrelevant: The role of interpersonal affect in task related ties. *Administrative Science Quarterly, 53*, 655–684.

49. Levi, D. (2014). *Group dynamics for teams*. Thousand Oaks, CA: Sage.

50. Wikipedia (2016). Social Loafing. Retrieved from https://en.wikipedia.org/wiki/Social_loafing

51. Karau, S. J., & Williams, K. D. (1993). Social loafing: A meta-analytic review and theoretical integration. *Journal of Personality and Social Psychology, 65(4)*, 681.

52. De Rond, M. (2012, August 6). Why less is more in teams. Retrieved from https://hbr.org/2012/08/why-less-is-more-in-teams/

53. Stillman, P., Gilovich, T. & Fujita, K. (2014). Predicting group outcomes from brief exposures. *Social Cognition, 32*, 71–82.

54. Filho, Edson, Gershon Tenenbaum, and Yanyun Yang. (2015). Cohesion, team mental models, and collective efficacy: Towards an integrated framework of team dynamics in sport. *Journal of Sports Sciences, 33(6)*, 641–653.

55. Mullen, B. and Copper, C. (1994). The relation between group cohesiveness and performance: An integration. *Psychological Bulletin, 115*, 210–227.

56. The Economist. (2000). The DaimlerChrysler emulsion. Retrieved from http://www.economist.com/node/341352

57. Mayer, R. C., Davis, J. H., & Schoorman, F. D. (1995). An integrative model of organizational trust. *Academy of Management Review, 20,* 709–734.

58. De Jong, B.A. & Elfring, T. (2010). How does trust affect the performance of ongoing teams? the mediating role of reflexivity, monitoring, and effort. Academy of Management Journal, 53, 535–549.

59. Mach, M., Dolan, S. & Tzafrir, S. (2010). The differential effect of team members' trust on team performance: The mediation role of team cohesion. *83, 771–794.*

60. Rozovsky, J. (2015, November 17). The five keys to a successful Google team. Retrieved from https://rework.withgoogle.com/blog/five-keys-to-a-successful-google-team/

61. Schmitt, E. (1987, April 1). Airlines stress team work in the cockpit. Retrieved 23 July 2016 from http://www.nytimes.com/1987/04/01/us/airlines-stress-team work-in-cockpit.html

62. Ford, J., Henderson, R. & O'Hare, D. (2014). The effects of crew resource management training on flight attendants' safety attitudes. *Journal of Safety Research, 48,* 49-56.

63. International Association of Fire Chiefs. (2003). Crew resource management: A positive change for the Fire Service. Retrieved from https://www.nh.gov/safety/divisions/fstems/ems/training/documents/crewmgt.pdf

64. Pentland, A. (2012). The new science of building great teams. *Harvard Business Review, 90,* 60–69.

65. Winsborough, D., & Marshall, B. (2007). Winsborough senior team benchmark report. Retrieved May 26, 2016 from http://bit.ly/1XVfELv

66. Janis, I. (1982). *Groupthink* (2nd ed.). Boston, MA: Houghton-Mifflin.

67. Bayne, D. (ND). Groupthink. Retrieved 23 July 2016 from http://danielbayn.com/groupthink/

68. Chamorro-Premuzic, T. (2015). *Confidence: The surprising truth about how much you need and how to get it.* London. Profile Books.

69. De Wit, F., Greer, L. & Jehn, K. (2012). The paradox of intragroup conflict: A meta-analysis. *Journal of Applied Psychology, 97(2)*, 360–390.

70. O'Neill, T., McLarnon, M., Hoffart, G., Woodley, H. & Allen, N. (2015). The structure and function of team conflict state profiles. *Journal of Management.* 1-26 Published online at http://journals.sagepub.com/doi/abs/10.1177/0149206315581662

71. DeDreu, C. & West, M. (2001). Minority dissent and team innovation: the importance of participation in decision making. *Journal of Applied Psychology, 86(6),*1191–1201.

72. Eisenhardt, K. M., Kahwajy, J. L., & Bourgeois, L. J. (2009). *How management teams can have a good fight.* Boston, Mass: Harvard Business Press.

73. Hackman, J., Wageman, R., & Fisher, C. M. (2009). Leading teams when the time is right: Finding the best moments to act. *Organizational Dynamics 38(3),* 192–203.

74. Curphy, G., & Hogan, R. T. (2012). *The Rocket Model: Practical advice for building high performing teams.* Tulsa, OK: Hogan Assessment Systems.

75. Chi, S.-P., Chang, Y.-Y., & Tsou, C.-M. (2012). The effect of team characteristics and communication environment to the virtual team performance. *International Journal of Networking and Virtual Organisations, 10*: 137-152

76. Andres, H. P. (2012). Technology-mediated collaboration, shared mental model and task performance. *Journal of Organizational and End User Computing, 24*: 64-81.

77. Brahm, T., & Kunze, F. (2012). The role of trust climate in virtual teams. *Journal of Managerial Psychology, 27*: 595-614.

78. Ruggieri, S. (2009). Leadership in virtual teams: A comparison of transformational and transactional leaders. *Social Behavior and Personality, 37*: 1017-1022.

79. Gilson, L. L., Maynard, M. T., Young, N. C. J., Vartiainen, M., & Hakonen, M. (2015). Virtual Teams Research: 10 Years, 10 Themes, and 10 Opportunities. *Journal of Management, 41(5),* 1313–1337.

80. Bell, S. T., & Brown, S. G. (2015). Selecting and composing cohesive teams. In E. Salas, W. B. Vessey, & A. X. Estrada (Eds.). *Team cohesion: Advances in psychological theory, methods and practice.* Bingley, UK: Emerald Group.

81. Woehr, D. J., Arciniega, L. M., & Poling, T. L. (2013). Exploring the effects of value diversity on team effectiveness. *Journal of Business Psychology, 28,* 107–121.

82. Kristof-Brown, A., Barrick, M. R., & Kay Stevens, C. (2005). When opposites attract: A multi-sample demonstration of complementary person–team fit on extraversion. *Journal of Personality, 73,* 935–958.

83. Ozer, D. J. & Martinez-Benet, V. (2006). Personality and the prediction of consequential outcomes. *Annual Review of Psychology. 57,* 401–21.

84. Roberts, B. W., Kuncel, N. R., Shiner, R., Caspi, A., & Goldberg, L. (2007). The power of personality: The comparative validity of personality traits, socioeconomic status and cognitive ability for predicting important life outcomes. *Perspectives on Psychological Science, 2,* 313–345.

85. Allport, G. W., & Odbert, H. S. (1936). Trait-names: A psycho-lexical study. *Psychological Monographs, 47,* 1–171.

86. Cattell, R. B. (1945). The description of personality: Principles and findings in a factor analysis. *American Journal of Psychology, 58,* 69–90.

87. Norman, W. T. (1963). Toward an adequate taxonomy of personality attributes: Replicated factor structure in peer nomination personality ratings. *Journal of Abnormal and Social Psychology, 66,* 574–583.

88. Roberts, B. W., & Bogg, T. (2004). A longitudinal study of the relationships between conscientiousness and the social-environmental factors and substance-use behaviors that influence health. *Journal of Personality, 72,* 325–353.

89. Hogan, R., & Roberts, B. W. (2004). A socioanalytic model of maturity. *Journal of Career Assessment, 12,* 207–217.

90. Rentfrow, P. J. (2010). Statewide differences in personality: Toward a psychological geography of the United States. *American Psychologist, 65*(6), 548–558.

91. Barrick, M. R., Stewart, G. L., Neubert, M. J., & Mount, M. K. (1998). Relating member ability and personality to work-team processes and team effectiveness. *The Journal of Applied Psychology, 83,* 377–391.

92. Bell, S. T. (2007). Deep-level composition variables as predictors of team performance: A meta-analysis. *The Journal of Applied Psychology, 92,* 595–615.

93. Liang, H-Y., Shih, H., & Chang, Y. (2015). Team diversity and team helping behavior: The mediating roles of team cooperation and team cohesion. *European Management Journal, 33,* 48–59.

94. Totterdell, P., Kellett, S., Teuchmann, K., & Briner, R. B. (1998). Evidence of mood linkage in work groups. *Journal of Personality and Social Psychology, 74(6)*, 1504–1515.

95. Felps, W., Mitchell, T. & Byington, E. (2006). How, when, and why bad apples spoil the barrel: Negative group members and dysfunctional groups. *Research in Organizational Behavior. 27*, 175–222.

96. Baumeister, R. F., Bratslavsky, E., Finkenauer, C., & Vohs, K. D. (2001). Bad is stronger than good. *Review of General Psychology, 5*, 323–370.

97. Gardner, N. (2007, February 12). Rotten to the core: How workplace "bad apples" spoil barrels of good employees. Retrieved from http://www.washington.edu/news/2007/02/12/rotten-to-the-core-how-workplace-bad-apples-spoil-barrels-of-good-employees/

98. Hogan, R. T., Chamorro-Premuzic, T., & Kaiser, R. B. (2013). Employability and career success: Bridging the gap between theory and reality. *Industrial and Organizational Psychology, 6*, 3–16.

99. Bell, S. T. (2007). Deep-level composition variables as predictors of team performance: A meta-analysis. *The Journal of Applied Psychology, 92*, 595–615.

100. Prewett, M. S., Walvoord, A. A. G., Stilson, F. R. B., Rossi, M. E., & Brannick, M. T. (2009). The team personality–team performance relationship revisited: The impact of criterion choice, pattern of workflow, and method of aggregation. *Human Performance, 22*, 273–296.

101. LePine, J. A. (2003). Team adaptation and post-change performance: Effects of team composition in terms of members' cognitive ability and personality. *The Journal of Applied Psychology, 88*, 27–39.

102. Homan, A. C., Hollenbeck, J. R., Humphrey, S. E., Van Knippenberg, D., Ilgen, D. R., & Van Kleef, G. A. (2008). Facing differences with an open mind: Openness to experience, salience of intragroup differences, and performance of diverse work groups. *Academy of Management Journal, 51*, 1204–1222.

103. LePine, J. A., Buckman, B. R., Crawford, E. R., & Methot, J. R. (2011). A review of research on personality in teams: Accounting for pathways spanning levels of theory and analysis. *Human Resource Management Review, 21(4)*, 311-330.

104. LePine, J. A., Buckman, B. R., Crawford, E. R., & Methot, J. R. (2011). A review of research on personality in teams: Accounting for pathways spanning levels of theory and analysis. *Human Resource Management Review, 21(4)*, 311-330.

105. Woolley, A., Aggarwal, I. & Malone, T. (2015). Collective intelligence and group performance. *Current Directions in Psychological Science, 24*, 420–424.

106. Cooke, N. (2015). Team cognition as interaction. *Current Directions in Psychological Science, 24*, 415–419.

107. Nettle, D. & Liddle, B. (2008). Agreeableness is related to social-cognitive, but not social-perceptual, theory of mind. *European Journal of Personality, 22*, 323–335.

108. Humphrey, S. E., Hollenbeck, J. R., Meyer, C. J., & Ilgen, D. (2011). Personality configurations in self-managed teams: A natural experiment on the effects of maximizing and minimizing variance in teams. *Journal of Applied Social Psychology, 41*, 1701–1732.

109. LePine, J. A. (2003). Team adaptation and post-change performance: Effects of team composition in terms of members' cognitive ability and personality. *Journal of Applied Psychology, 88, 27–39.*

110. Prewett, M. S., Walvoord, A. A. G., Stilson, F. R. B., Rossi, M. E., & Brannick, M. T. (2009). The team personality–team performance relationship revisited: The impact of criterion choice, pattern of workflow, and method of aggregation. *Human Performance, 22,* 273–296.

111. Ancona, D. G., & Caldwell, D. F. (1992). Demography and design: Predictors of new product team performance. *Organization Science, 3,* 321–341.

112. Holland, J. L. (1997). *Making vocational choices: A theory of vocational personalities and work environments* (3rd ed.). Odessa, FL: Psychological Assessment Resources.

113. Schneider, B., Goldstein, H. W., & Smith, B. (1995). The ASA framework: An update. *Personnel Psychology, 48,* 747–773.

114. Woehr, D., Arcieniega, L., & Poling, T. (2013). Exploring the effects of value diversity on team effectiveness. *Journal of Business Psychology, 28,* 107–121.

115. Chou, L. F., Wang, A. C., Wang, T. Y., Huang, M. P., & Cheng, B. S. (2008). Shared work values and team member effectiveness: The mediation of trustfulness and trustworthiness. *Human Relations, 61,* 1713–1742.

116. Adams, H. A. (2009). Effective transformation teams: The influence of values and transformational leadership. Paper presented at the *16th EDAMBA Summer Academy,* Sorenze, France.

117. Cali Cartel. (2016). In *Wikipedia.* Retrieved September 7 2016 from https://en.wikipedia.org/wiki/Cali_Cartel

118. Jehn, K. A., Northcraft, G. B., & Neale, M. A. (1999). Why differences make a difference: A field study of diversity, conflict, and performance in work groups. *Administrative Science Quarterly, 44,* 741–763.

119. Van Vugt, M., Hart, C., & Leader, T. (2008). Does stability foster team performance? A European football (soccer) inquiry. Unpublished manuscript. Retrieved from http://www.professormarkvanvugt.com/publications/25-articles/applications/88-does-stability-foster-team-performance-2008.html

120. Hogan, R., & Hogan, J. (2001). Assessing leadership: A view from the dark side. *International Journal of Selection and Assessment, 9,* 40–51.

121. Kaiser, R.B. (2016). Dealing with the dark side. *Talent Quarterly,* 8, 37-42.

122. Winsborough, D. L., & Sambath, V. (2013). Not like us: An investigation into the personalities of New Zealand CEOs. *Consulting Psychology Journal: Practice and Research, 65*(2), 87–107.

123. Ilies, R., Wagner, D. T., & Morgeson, F. P. (2007). Explaining affective linkages in teams: individual differences in susceptibility to contagion and individualism-collectivism. *The Journal of Applied Psychology, 92*(4), 1140–1148.

124. Meyer, B., Glenz, A., Antino, M., & Rico, R. (2014). Faultlines and subgroups : A meta-review and measurement guide. *Small Group Research, 45*(6), 633 –670.

125. Thatcher, S. M. B., & Patel, P. C. (2012). Group faultlines: A review, integration, and guide to future research. *Journal of Management, 38*(4), 969–1009.

126. Mäs, M., Flache, A., Takács, K., & Jehn, K. A. (2013). In the short term we divide, in the long term we unite: Demographic crisscrossing and the effects of faultlines on sub-group polarization. *Organization Science, 3,* 716-736

127. This is a real case although the name of the agency has been changed.

128. Zimbardo, P.G. (2007). *The Lucifer Effect: Understanding How Good People Turn Evil*. New York: Random House.

129. Reicher, S., & Haslam, S. A. (2006). Rethinking the psychology of tyranny: the BBC prison study. *The British Journal of Social Psychology*, *45*, 1–40;. See also: The BBC prison experiment. Retrieved from http://www.bbcprisonstudy.org/index.php

130. Bryant, A. (2010). Does your team have the four essential types? Interview with Paul Maritz, president and CEO of VMware. *New York Times,* October 10. Retrieved from http://www.nytimes.com/2010/10/03/business/03corner.html?_r=1

131. Forer, B.R. (1949). The fallacy of personal validation: A classroom demonstration of gull-ibility. *Journal of Abnormal and Social Psychology*, *44 (1)*: 118–123.

132. Furnham, A. (2005), *The psychology of behaviour at work: the individual in the organiza-tion*, Psychology Press, Hove.

133. Fisher, S. G., Hunter, T. a., & Macrosson, W. D. K. (2001). A validation study of Belbin's team roles. *European Journal Of Work And Organizational Psychology*, *10*, 121–144

134. Grant, A. (2013) Say goodbye to the MBTI, the fad that won't die. Retrieved from https://www.linkedin.com/pulse/20130917155206-69244073-say-goodbye-to-mbti-the-fad-that-won-t-die

135. Bess, T.L. & Harvey, R.J. (2001). Bimodal score distributions and the MBTI: Fact or artifact? Paper presented at the Annual Conference of the Society for Industrial and Organizational Psychology, San Diego 2001.

136. Burnett, D. (2013). Nothing Personal: The questionable science of the Myers Briggs Test. Retrieved from https://www.theguardian.com/science/brain-flapping/2013/mar/19/myers-briggs-test-unscientific

137. Pittenger, D. J. (2005). Cautionary comments regarding the Myers-Briggs Type Indicator. *Consulting Psychology Journal: Practice and Research*, *57*, 210–221

138. Hogan, R.T. (2007). *Personality and the fate of organizations*. Mahwah, NJ: Lawrence Erlbaum Associates.

139. Furnham, A. (1992). *Personality at work: The role of individual differences in the work-place*. London: Routledge. See also: Furnham, A., Steele, H., & Pendleton, D. (1993). A psychometric assessment of the Belbin Team-Role Self-Perception Inventory. *Journal of Occupational and Organizational Psychology*, *66*, 245-257.

140. Benne and Sheats' Group Roles (2016). Retrieved 16 September from https://www.mindtools.com/pages/article/newTMM_85.htm

141. Hogan, J., & Holland, B. (2003). Using theory to evaluate personality and job-perfor-mance relations: a socioanalytic perspective. *The Journal of Applied Psychology*, 88(1), 100–112. http://doi.org/10.1037/0021-9010.88.1.100

142. Bruce, J. M., Hancock, L. M., Arnett, P., & Lynch, S. (2010). Treatment adherence in mul-tiple sclerosis: Association with emotional status, personality, and cognition. *Journal of Behavioral Medicine*, 33(3), 219–227.

143. Roberts, B. W., Kuncel, N. R., Shiner, R., Caspi, A., & Goldberg, L. R. (2007). The power of personality: The comparative validity of personality traits, socioeconomic status, and cognitive ability for predicting important life outcomes. *Perspectives on Psychological Science*, *2(4)*, 313–345.

144. Parker, G. M. (1990), *Team players and teamwork: The competitive business strategy*. Jossey-Bass, Oxford.

145. Langvik, E. (2006). Personality traits and team roles: Introducing a tricolor model of team roles and its relationship to the personality traits in the five factor model. Poster presented at the 13th European Conference on Personality, Athens, Greece.

146. Hollenbeck, J. R., DeRue, D. S., & Guzzo, R. (2004). Bridging the gap between I/O research and HR practice: Improving team composition, team training, and team task design. *Human Resource Management, 43(4)*, 353–366.

147. Takala, J., Hämäläinen, P., Saarela, K. L., Yun, L. Y., Manickam, K., Jin, T. W. & Lin, G. S. (2014). Global Estimates of the Burden of Injury and Illness at Work in 2012. *Journal of Occupational and Environmental Hygiene, 11(5)*, 326–337.

148. Lencioni, P. (2002). *The five dysfunctions of a team: A leadership fable*. San Francisco: Jossey-Bass.

149. Curphy, G. J., & Hogan, R. (2012*). The rocket model: Practical advice for building high performing teams*. Tulsa, OK: Hogan Press.

150. Dunning, D., Heath, C., & Suls, J. M. (2004). Flawed self-assessment implications for health, education, and the workplace. *Psychological Science in the Public Interest, 5*, 69–106.

151. http://employerlawreport.default.wp1.lexblog.com/files/2013/09/Hudgens.pdf

152. These tables have been adapted from: Shuffler, M. L., DiazGranados, D., & Salas, E. (2011). There's a science for that: Team development interventions in organizations. *Current Directions in Psychological Science, 20(6)*, 365–372.

153. Noguchi, N. (2014, July 8). Paintballing the boss: Office team-building exercises gone bad. Retrieved from http://www.npr.org/2014/07/08/329527787/paintballing-the-boss-office-team-building-exercises-gone-bad

154. Klein, C., DiazGranados, D., Salas, E., Le, H., Burke, C. S., Lyons, R., & Goodwin, G. F. (2009). Does team building work? *Small Group Research, 40(2)*, 181–222.

155. Shuffler ML, DiazGranados D, Salas E: There's a science for that: Team development interventions in organizations. *Current Directions in Psychological Science, 20(6)*, 365–372.

156. Edmondson, A. (2012). *Teaming: How organizations learn, innovate and compete in the innovation economy*. John Wiley, San Francisco.

157. Delise, L., Gorman, C.A., Brooks, A.M., Rentsch, J.R., & Steele- Johnson, D. (2010). The effects of team training on team out- comes: A meta-analysis. *Performance Improvement Quarterly, 22*, 53–80.

158. Demmitt, J. (2015, November 6).This startup wants to help business hire entire developer teams away from other companies. Retrieved from http://www.geekwire.com/2015/this-startup-wants-to-make-poaching-entire-developer-teams-as-simple-as-possible/

159. Chamorro-Premuzic, T. (2016). *The talent delusion: Why data not intuition is the key to unlocking human potential*. Little Brown, London.

160. Kemery, E., Bedeian, A., Mossholder, K. & Touliatos, J. (1985). Outcomes of role stress: A multisample constructive replication. *Academy of Management Review, 28*, 363-375.

161. Staats, C. (2014). State of the science: Implicit bias review 2014. *The Psychologist, 27*, 390–397.

162. Darling, M., Parry, C., & Moore, J. (2005). Learning in the thick of it. *Harvard Business Review, 85*, 84–92.

ABOUT THE AUTHOR
DAVE WINSBOROUGH

Dave Winsborough is an English-born New Zealand psychologist. Originally as a clinician, he became interested in the way people behaved in groups. As a result of this interest, he developed original measures and techniques to explore team dynamics and performance. He is the author of numerous scientific papers, book chapters and articles. Currently based in New York as head of innovation for Hogan Assessments, Dave is founder and Chairman of New Zealand's largest organizational psychology consulting firm.

Made in the USA
Lexington, KY
06 August 2019